Bosewitz / Kleinschroth
Better Your Business English

Dr. René Bosewitz ist Native Speaker und bereitet in einer deutschen Zweigstelle der London Chamber of Commerce Firmenangehörige auf einschlägige sprachliche Prüfungen vor. Er trainiert zudem seit vielen Jahren Manager aus Banken und Industrie in Business English (mehr Informationen unter www.combenations.de). Er hat u. a. *Better Your English* und *Perfect Your English* sowie zusammen mit Robert Kleinschroth *Joke Your Way Through English Grammar* und *Joke by Joke to Conversation* veröffentlicht.

Robert Kleinschroth unterrichtet Englisch am Gymnasium und an der Universität Heidelberg. Er hat zwanzig Jahre Praxis in der Erwachsenenbildung und leitete fünfzehn Jahre lang die Sprachabteilung eines Großunternehmens. Robert Kleinschroth hat zusammen mit Anne-Laure und Dieter Maupai *Flüssiges Französisch* verfasst und außerdem *Sprachen lernen* geschrieben.

RENÉ BOSEWITZ/ROBERT KLEINSCHROTH

BETTER YOUR BUSINESS ENGLISH

CRASHPROGRAMM ZUM MEISTERN TYPISCHER PROBLEME

Anaconda

Die Deutsche Nationalbibliothek verzeichnet diese Publikation in der Deutschen Nationalbibliografie; detaillierte bibliografische Daten sind im Internet unter http://dnb.d-nb.de abrufbar.

Überarbeitete und aktualisierte Neuausgabe Februar 2009

Umschlaggestaltung: Druckfrei. Dagmar Herrmann, Köln
Printed in Czech Republic 2009
ISBN 978-3-86647-315-7
www.anacondaverlag.de
info@anaconda-verlag.de

FOCUS: on business skills and cross-cultural topics

PHRASES
Master your phrases

B*etter your business English* lädt Sie ein zu einem Streifzug durch typische Situationen des Geschäftsalltags. Die kurzen Dialoge kreisen um Themen wie Vorstellungsgespräch, Geschäftsreise, Mieten eines Autos, Vereinbarung eines Termins, Besprechung und Präsentation, um nur einige zu nennen. Mit jedem Kapitel erweitern Sie Ihr Business English und lernen wichtige Redewendungen, um die jeweilige Situation zu meistern.

Kernstück eines jeden Kapitels sind die peinlichen Fehler, die unserem deutschen Helden immer wieder unterlaufen. Sie werden diese Fehler gar nicht erst machen. Unsere Übungen sollen Sie davor bewahren. Und Sie werden dabei auch oft etwas zu schmunzeln haben. Wir haben das Übungsmaterial mit viel Liebe ausgesucht. Es besteht fast immer aus kurzen *jokes* oder geistreichen Zitaten.

Übrigens, haben Sie es bemerkt? *Better your business English* klingt wie Englisch, ist es aber nicht. Richtig wäre: *Better business English* oder *Improve your business English*. Wussten Sie schon, dass *Kommission* nicht *commission*, *Provision* nicht *provision* und *Defekt* nicht *defect* heißt? Um solche Probleme geht es in diesem Buch – aber nicht nur um die falschen Freunde des englischen Wortschatzes. Da sind auch noch die grammatischen und kulturellen Klippen, die es sicher zu umschiffen gilt. Auch dabei will Ihnen das Buch helfen.

Am Ende der Kapitel informieren Sie kurze Texte über so nützliche Dinge wie das geschickte Verhalten in Bewerbungsgesprächen, das professionelle Abfassen eines Lebenslaufs, den Stil von Präsentationen, *smalltalk* und *networking* und vieles mehr.

Für das Lernen zu zweit oder in Gruppen finden Sie Anregungen unter *Classroom activities*. Zum Schluss laden wir Sie zu einem Abschlusstest ein: *Top 30 mistakes quiz*.

Wir wünschen Ihnen viel Spaß und Erfolg bei der Lektüre.

1 Chapter THE COMPANY*: HOW IT ALL BEGAN

Once upon a time there was a sleepy little university town in the south of Germany called Highdelmountain. Located there was an active medium-sized company specialised in manufacturing medical equipment. "The times they are changing" as the song goes and there was the chance of a merger or *at last* a joint enterprise with a British company, MEDIMAKE, who are in almost the same field. This would be an excellent opportunity for MEDIQUIP, the German manufacturer, to get a foothold in the lucrative British market, at the same time exchanging know-how and perhaps developing synergies.
The top managements of the two companies came together to plan their initial strategies. That was the easy part. All well and good, but first there has to be communication with the potential partner at lower levels, too. The idea of the merger or joint venture has to be sold. An envoy has to go to the UK to smooth over fears, to show the advantages and to set the scene for later co-operation. And it should be a flexible, *sensible* colleague, fluent in English and highly motivated. Who should that be? The Board at MEDIQUIP have a short list of candidates. A good candidate might be Dr Uwe Tissmann, Head of Research at MEDIQUIP, year-long participant in the English courses of Professor Busyjoke of Com-be-nations, Highdelmountain, and an intelligent, but also ambitious employee. But it's all not as easy as that. Let's follow the story.

A thank-you letter to MEDIQUIP

Dear Sirs,
For twenty years I was totally deaf, and after using your hearing aid HA66 for only ten days I heard from a long-lost cousin in Eriwan.

ATTENTION, PLEASE!

There are two things to improve in the text.
We've marked them in *italics*. Can you correct them?

* Witziges und Nützliches zum Thema Company English in *Build up Your Word Power. Wortschatztraining on the Job,* rororo sprachen.

TASK 1: Business key words

Remember these phrases? Can you complete them?

sich spezialisieren auf	specialise ____________
medizinische Geräte herstellen	____________ medical equipment
gemeinsames Projekt	joint ____________
in der gleichen Branche sein	be in the same ____________
die Gelegenheit, etwas zu tun	the ____________ to do something
auf dem Markt Fuß fassen	get a ____________ in the market
Fachwissen austauschen	____________ know-how
Synergieeffekte entwickeln	____________ synergies
ein möglicher Partner	a ____________ partner
die Voraussetzungen für eine Zusammenarbeit schaffen	____________ the scene for co-operation
Befürchtungen ausräumen	____________ over fears
eine engere Auswahl an Kanditaten	a ____________ of candidates
jemanden in die engere Auswahl für eine Stelle nehmen	shortlist somebody ____________ a job

TASK 2: Test your memory

1. Do you remember why MEDIQUIP was interested in a merger?
2. Why was it necessary to send an envoy to Britain?
3. What qualifications and characteristics are necessary to do this job?

TASK 3: Pitfalls for Germans

Here are the two things to correct.
See also Task 6.

1. There was the chance of a merger or *at last* a joint enterprise with a British company.
2. Dr Uwe Tissmann, ... a *sensible*, but also ambitious employee.

TASK 4: Describing MEDIQUIP

Fit the words into the right place and in their correct form:

diversify	*diversifizieren*	needs	*Bedürfnisse*
requirement	*Anforderungen*	found	*gründen*
subsidiary	*Tochtergesellschaft*	supplier	*Lieferant*
innovate	*erneuern*	range	*Produktreihe*
market leader	*Marktführer*	grow	*wachsen*
attention	*Aufmerksamkeit*	employ	*beschäftigen*
breakthrough	*Durchbruch*	operation	*Tätigkeit*

MEDIQUIP is one of Germany's leading ____________________ of medical equipment. The company __________________ over 300 people and has ____________________________ located in ten cities. It has become the _____________ ________________ within 40 years. The company was ____________________ in 1960 and its principal _______________ were in the orthodontic field. Since then the company has _____________________ rapidly to meet the ____________________ of both the dental and surgical sector.

The company has always recognised the _________________ of changing market needs and has _________________ and ___________________ its product _______________ in time. The _______________ came with the microchip. The computerised pace-maker has become the company's cash cow. Believe it or not, the hearing-aids and ultrasound scanners even caught the _______________ of various secret services and military leaders.

TASK 5: Remember the product?

_____________ a small device that makes sounds louder and helps a deaf person to hear.

_____________ a device to produce a picture of the inside of a person's body on a computer screen.

_____________ an electronic device placed under the skin near the heart to make the heart beat more regularly.

TASK 6: Joke your way round trouble spots

Is it A or B?

1. After Christmas the department stores were crowded with people trying to exchange the Christmas presents they didn't like. A disguested husband shouted to his wife, "Won't you ______________ keep the baby?"

   A at least **B** at last

2. Most laws seem ________________ until policemen try to enforce them against nice people like us.

   A reasonable **B** sensitive

3. The proprietor of a highly successful optician's was instructing his son as to how to get the best price.
   "Son," he said, "be __________________ to your customer's reactions. After you have fitted the glasses, and the customer asks what the charge will be, you say, 'The price is a hundred dollars.' Then pause and wait to see if he flinches. If he does not flinch you continue, '... for the frames. The lenses will be another hundred dollars.' Then you pause again, this time only slightly, and watch for the flinch. If the customer does not flinch this time, you add firmly '... each'."

   A sensitive **B** sensible

How they make a profit

A visitor who was being shown round MEDIQUIP asked his guide, "But if it costs 150 Euros to make these hearing-aids and you sell them for 150 Euros, where does the profit come in?" – "From repairing them," said the guide.

FOCUS: Describing yourself

One year ago Dr Tissmann felt that his present job at MEDIQUIP wasn't challenging him enough (that's another reason why he wanted to go to England), so he applied to Heighst, a major pharmaceutical company. Below you will find his CV or resumé.

Curriculum Vitae

Personal details

Name:	Dr Uwe Tissmann
Address:	Kleinschmidtstrasse 13, 69115 Heidelberg, Germany
Telephone:	06221 27555
Date of Birth:	10/10/55

Work experience

Present employment

1992 – present:	Director of R&D division at MEDIQUIP, designing new products, improving test procedures, organising restructuring of division.
1988 – 1992:	Full time research position at Freecastle University, preparing for doctorate. Created new test series for medical equipment. Successfully co-ordinated teaching schedule for undergraduate students.
1986 – 1988:	Applied for entry to marketing diploma in the UK. Completed research and dissertation at Manchester University (M.Sc.). Subject: technical marketing in the medical equipment sector. Successfully launched a product on the UK market as part of a project.
1982 – 1986:	Was accepted at Dusselvillage University as an undergraduate in the Medical Faculty. Specialised in Human Medicine. Course completed October, 1986.
1984 – 1986:	Participated in a training course as a commercial clerk at Bagger AG.

Formal Qualifications

1981: Obtained "A" levels in biology, chemistry, Latin, English
1986: Diploma in Medicine, University of Dusselvillage
1988: M.Sc. in Marketing, University of Manchester, UK
1992: Doctorate, Freecastle University, subject "Testing Medical Equipment".

Other Qualifications and Experience

London Chamber of Commerce, English for Marketing Diploma, 1988
Knowledge of languages: English fluent
French intermediate

Essentials of your curriculum vitae

A. The aim of a CV

- A CV provides a summary of your education, training and work experience to date in the space of one or two pages of A4 paper.
- A good CV conveys all the reasons why an employer should want to know more about you. It excites interest by showing clearly that you are someone who can offer skills and personal qualities.
- The essential aim of your CV is to interest an employer sufficiently to open the door to the next stage of the recruitment process. CVs alone won't get you a job, but they must beat off most of the competition, which for some jobs can be fierce.

B. The content of the CV

1. Personal details

- name, address and telephone number are sufficient
- if the advertisement specifies an age limit, include your date of birth

2. Work experience

- start with your most recent employment
- state the period during which you worked for each employer (month and year)
- the reason for leaving is not normally included in CVs
- give the name of each company and its location (not full address); put your job title for each
- itemise your main responsibilities and duties; give most details for the most recent employers
- it's essential to include the achievements and accomplishments that are relevant to the job you're applying for
- professional memberships, etc.
- include any other accomplishments relevant to your profession, such as special awards or distinctions

3. Education and training

- details of any training or course of study since leaving formal education
- name of college or university and years of attendance, qualification and subject
- don't include evening classes and courses attended for personal interests unless they are directly relevant to the job

C. The language of the CV

Your CV should contain short, abbreviated descriptions and not necessarily full sentences. Follow these guidelines:

- avoid the first person 'I'
- eliminate as many other words as you can (like 'the' and 'that'), unless they change (the) meaning or readability
- try to start each item with a verb – this makes the point that you're actively doing and achieving things in your work
- use adverbs to convey how activities were performed;
  instead of
  My responsibilities included training staff in new customer-care procedures, change to
  Successfully trained staff in new customer-care procedures

Use words for success and results

increased	improved	successfully
identified	reduced	established
developed	initiated	negotiated
produced	launched	achieved
designed	motivated	co-ordinated
organised	saved	created

Don't write	Write
worked on customer service programme	improved service to customers
dealt with suppliers	negotiated better terms with suppliers, saving 15 per cent on costs
business development	recognised potential for growth in new sector
clerical work	established improved administrative systems

WORD AID

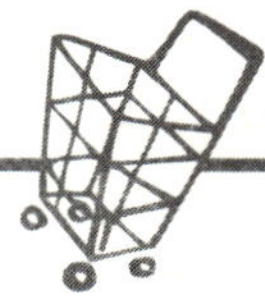

"A" level	*Abitur*
abbreviate	*abkürzen*
accomplishment	*Leistung; Fertigkeit*
achievement	*Leistung*
age limit	*Altersgrenze*
ambitious	*ehrgeizig*
apply to	*anwenden auf*
apply for	*sich bewerben für*
at last	*endlich*
at least	*wenigstens*
attendance	*Besuch (von Schulen etc.)*
avoid	*vermeiden*

award	*Preis, Auszeichnung*
beat off the competition	*die Konkurrenz schlagen*
cash cow	*Goldesel*
charge	*hier: Preis*
clerical work	*Büroarbeit*
commercial clerk	*Industriekaufmann*
contain	*enthalten*
convey	*vermitteln*
customer service	*Kundendienst*
customer-care procedures	*Methoden der Kundenbetreuung*
CV	*Lebenslauf*
deaf	*taub*
dental sector	*zahnmedizinischer Sektor*
dentist	*Zahnarzt*
department store	*Warenhaus*
design	*entwerfen*
device	*Gerät*
disgusted	*angeekelt, schockiert*
distinction	*Auszeichnung*
employment	*Anstellung*
enforce a law	*ein Gesetz durchführen*
envoy	*Gesandter*
essential; the ~ aim	*das Hauptziel*
establish	*einrichten*
excite interest	*Interesse erregen*
fierce competition	*scharfe Konkurrenz*
flinch	*zucken; Zucken*
fluent; be ~ in English	*fließend Englisch sprechen*
foothold; get a ~ in a market	*auf einem Markt Fuß fassen*
formal education	*Schulbildung*
frame	*Gestell; Rahmen*
guidelines	*Richtlinien*
hearing-aid	*Hörgerät*
improve	*verbessern*
initial strategies	*Anfangsstrategien*
initiate	*initiieren, anbahnen*
intermediate level	*Grundkenntnisse*
item	*Punkt, Frage*

joint enterprise	*gemeinsames Unternehmen*
launch a product	*ein Produkt auf den Markt bringen*
located	*gelegen*
location	*geographische Lage*
long-lost; a ~ cousin	*ein verschollener Vetter*
manufacturer	*Fabrikant, Hersteller*
medical equipment	*medizinische Geräte*
medium-sized	*von mittlerer Größe*
merger	*Firmenzusammenschluss; Fusion*
negotiate	*verhandeln*
opportunity	*günstige Gelegenheit*
orthodontic; in the ~ field	*auf zahnmedizinischem Gebiet*
participant	*Teilnehmer*
proprietor	*Eigentümer*
provide a summary	*eine Zusammenfassung geben*
readability	*Lesbarkeit*
reasonable	*vernünftig*
recent	*kürzlich*
recruitment process	*Einstellungsverfahren*
research	*Forschung*
responsibility	*Verantwortung*
save	*sparen; retten*
sensible	*vernünftig*
sensitive	*sensibel, einfühlsam*
set the scene for	*den Schauplatz vorbereiten*
smooth over fears	*Befürchtungen zerstreuen*
sufficient	*ausreichend*
teaching schedule	*Lehrplan*
test procedures	*Prüfverfahren*
undergraduate student	*Student in der Ausbildung*

Time for a smile

Dentist: Stop screaming! I haven't even touched your tooth. In fact, you're not even on the chair yet.

Boy: I know, but you're standing on my foot!

2 Chapter THE INTERVIEW

Doing a good interview is not easy. It's also just as difficult for the interviewer to ask the right questions as it is for the interviewee to give suitable answers. To say something, but not too much, to be firm, but not arrogant is difficult to achieve.
The task of the interviewer is to find out whether the candidate is able to fit into a team. He or she might have the best qualifications, but be totally incapable of integrating into a department. Sometimes it can be like Russian roulette. Find a few guidelines on our focus page.

The right candidate

An applicant was interviewed for a marketing position. "What we are looking for," said the personnel manager, "is a man of vision, a man with drive, determination and courage, a man who never quits, who can inspire others, in short – a man who can pull the company's football team up from the bottom of the league."

ATTENTION, PLEASE!

There are four things to improve in the dialogue.
We've marked them in *italics*. Can you correct them?
See Task 3: Pitfalls for Germans.

Presenting oneself

Dr Kleinshirt (K), member of the Board at MEDIQUIP, is interviewing our hero, Dr Tissmann (T). He doesn't know the fellow well, only by sight and has to find out whether this person has the fine touch needed to "sell" a really positive merger. But how to decide that? Of course, this conversation went on in German, but you have to use your imagination!

K: Do sit down, Dr Tissmann. Of course I know your name and your face, but I have *to learn to know* the person in more detail. The company's grown so much.

T: Yes, of course, if you'll permit me, I'll just *remember* you of my activities until now. I've been at MEDIQUIP for eight years. In the R&D department. I've been doing basic research for all our product ranges.

K: Yes, yes, of course, I am aware of that. But what originally brought you to MEDIQUIP?

T: I studied medicine for my first degree. And then I did a postgraduate qualification in marketing. So obviously my career was to be in medical technology of some sort.

K: And that brought you to us.

T: Yes, I'm an ambitious sort of fellow and I went for the best. I consider MEDIQUIP to be a torch-bearer in this field.

K: Well, I'm glad you feel like that. About this work in England, don't you feel it might be expecting a lot of an employee coming from here, to deal with another culture?

T: Of course, but if I might describe my own personality a little, I'm a person who needs a challenge.

K: In what way would this PR type job bring you out of your reserves?

T: Well, first I'd have to have a complete overview of our products from a technical point of view. And then I'd compare ...

K: I know you're able to do all that. What interests me more are your interpersonal skills. What makes you think you can handle the psychological problems that come with the culture clash? Englishmen and Germans are different in their behaviour. And what about the situation that we are *overtaking* their company?

T: Well, what you say is true, absolutely true. And these problems do exist, especially for us Germans. *It's my meaning* that we have not to be too pushy, we have to listen, to understand other people's positions. And I guess we have to choose our words carefully. It's a difficult situation for them. We've got to get them on our side.

K: And how do you propose to do that?

T: I would try to build networks, to know them socially. My first priority would be to connect with them mentally, to find out how they work and think.

K: Okay. Leave it with me. I may get back to you.

TASK 1: Key words in business

Medizin studieren	______ a degree in medicine
Grundlagenforschung betreiben	do basic ______________
Produktreihen	product ______________
Medizintechnik	______________ technology
Vorreiter auf einem Gebiet	a torch-bearer in a _________
viel von jemandem erwarten	___________ a lot of someone
eine Herausforderung benötigen	need a ______________
mit einem Problem umgehen können	be able to ___________ a problem
eine Firma übernehmen	_________ a company _______
Geschick im Umgang mit Menschen	________________ skills
ein Netz (persönlicher Beziehungen) aufbauen	______________ a network

TASK 2: Test your memory

1. How long has Tissmann been at MEDIQUIP and what have his activities been?
2. How does Tissmann characterise himself?
3. What skills does the new job most require?

Great expectations

Young Ronny applied to a big advertising company for a part-time job. The personnel manager, wanting to test Ronny asked, "My boy, what would you do with a million pounds?" – "Well, sir," replied Ronny, "I wasn't expecting that much at the beginning."

TASK 3: Pitfalls for Germans

There are four things to improve in the text.

1. I have *to learn to know* the person in more detail.
2. What about the situation that we are *overtaking* their company?
3. *It's my meaning* that we have not to be too pushy.
4. I'll just *remember* you of my activities until now.

TASK 4: Joke your way round trouble spots

One word in German – three words in English

brauchen	need take require

1. How many psychiatrists does it ________ to change a light bulb? – Only one. But the bulb must want to be changed.
2. It's the final proof of God's omnipotence that he ________ not exist in order to save us.
3. It ________ a lot of experience for a girl to kiss like a beginner.
4. To err is human, but to really foul things up ________ a computer.

TASK 5: Another trouble spot to joke around

One word in German – two words in English

erinnern	remind remember

1. Last words of a speaker: "Now that we've all enjoyed a wonderful meal, I' d like to ________________ you that wild, uninhibited applause burns up twenty-five calories a minute! So start burning! Cheers."
2. By the time you reach 75 years of age you've learnt everything. All you have to do is to try and ________________ it.

3. Only when the final draft of the document has been typed up and printed will the boss _______________ an important point that must be added to the middle of it.
4. I can't seem to _______________ your name, and please don't _______________ me!

TASK 6: Beef up your word power

Replace the words in *italics* with those used in the text.

1. If you'll *allow* me ...
2. And how do you *suggest doing* that?
3. My first priority would be to *get in touch* with them mentally.
4. I have to get to know the person *better.*

TASK 7: Spot the mistake

1. I am at MEDIQUIP for eight years.
2. I have studied medicine for my first degree.
3. And then I have done a postgraduate qualification in marketing.

TASK 8: Writing a CV

First, read these notes.

1. Left school. Went to Italy for six months to study architecture.
2. Returned to England. Then applied for three-year architectural course.
3. Studying at Manchester University, developed an interest in photography.
4. Left the university in April 1993. Didn't take my final exams in June.
5. Worked for advertising agency. Saved enough money.
6. Qualified. Have been employed by the Daily News.
7. Contract finishes in March. Shall be immediately available to start new job.

Now it's your turn. The first has been done for you.
Use the words in the box to link up these sentences.

after	when	as soon as	since	while	before	until

(1) *After leaving school in 1976, I went to Italy for six months* to study architecture.

(2) ____________ I returned to England, I applied for a three-year architectural course.

(3) ____________ I was studying at Manchester University, I developed an interest in photography.

(4) I left the university in April 1993, ____________ taking my final exams in June and came to London.

(5) I worked for an advertising agency ____________ I had enough money to start a two-year diploma course in photography at Hamden College of Fine Arts which I completed in 1997.

(6) ____________ qualifying, I have been employed as a sports photographer by the Daily News.

(7) However, ____________ my contract finishes in March, I shall be available to start a new job immediately.

Yours sincerely JAMES STEWART

FOCUS: The interview for a job

A. Preparations for the interview

- Find out, if you can, who will be interviewing you and check the physical layout of the room.
- Before the interview ask for information about the job and, if possible, have a chat informally about it with someone in the organisation.
- Don't worry if you do not pick up everything the interviewer tells you about the job at the start. Ask detailed questions later.
- A common way of starting off the interview is to take candidates through their application forms.
- Be aware of the purpose of questions about qualifications. Are they meant to relax or to probe?
- Talk about your qualifications in a positive way and show how they are relevant to the job.

B. The structure of the interview

1. Ice-Breakers to make you feel at ease

- Welcome and thank you for coming. I see you've brought good weather with you.
- Have you had a good journey?
- Did you drive over?
- Tell me a little about yourself.

2. Questions to find out if you can do the job

- What qualifications do you have for the job?
- What experience do you feel you can bring to the job?
- Describe the main areas of responsibility in your present job
- What can you offer the company?
- Why do you want to work for us?
- Why should I offer you the job?
- What have you achieved in your present job?
- What are you good at?
- What do you find most difficult?

3. Questions to find out if you really want to do the job

- Tell me what you know about our company.
- Why do you want the job?
- How do you see yourself five years from now?
- What do you enjoy most about the work you do?
- What do you enjoy least?
- Why did you leave your last job?
- This job involves a much higher level of responsibility than your current one. How do you feel about that?
- As senior project manager, what would you see as your main aims?

4. Questions to find out if you will fit

- How do you feel about taking instructions from someone?
- Give an example of how you resolved a difficulty with another member of staff.
- Give an example of a time when you worked as a member of a team.
- How do you see yourself fitting in here?

MAGIC Squares

Match the jokes with the words. Put the right numbers in the squares below. All columns and rows will add up to the same number, 15.

Entschuldigen: *apologise* or *excuse*?
Machen: *get, make, take, do* or *hold*?
Fahren: *go* or *drive*?

1. excuse	**2.** take	**3.** make
4. get	**5.** held	**6.** do
7. drive	**8.** went	**9.** apologise

A. Education is when you read the fine print. Experience is what you ___ if you don't.

B. "Officer," said the sweet young girl coming into the police station, "where do I ___ for shooting my husband?"

C. A taxpayer is someone who doesn't have to ___ a civil service exam to work for the government.

D. Written on the door of the biology classroom: ___ love – not war. See the teacher for details.

E. If more than one person can be ___ responsible, nobody will be found to blame.

F. Sign in a bar: If you suddenly notice our colour TV – don't ___. It's black and white.

G. Did you hear about the Scot who won a holiday for two in Majorca? He ___ by himself twice.

H. ___ me, Mr Smith, but who wrote this nonsense into your manuscript?

I. "I've prepared the turkey," said Ron to his Anne. "I've plucked it and stuffed it. All you've got to ___ is kill it and cook it."

A =	**B =**	**C =**
D =	**E =**	**F =**
G =	**H =**	**I =**

WORD AID

achieve	*leisten; vollbringen*
ambitious	*ehrgeizig*
applicant	*Bewerber*
application form	*Bewerbungsformular*
apply to	*sich bewerben bei*
at ease; feel ~ ~	*sich wohl fühlen*
available	*verfügbar; vorhanden*
basic / pure research	*Grundlagenforschung*
be aware of …	*Vorsicht vor …*
be forced back on one's resources	*auf sich selbst gestellt werden*
bottom; the ~ of the league	*der letzte Tabellenplatz*
challenge	*Herausforderung*
congregation	*Gemeinde*
culture clash	*Aufeinanderprallen von Kulturen*
deal with another culture	*mit anderen Kulturen zu tun haben*
depth; know in ~	*genau kennen*
determination	*Entschlossenheit*
do a postgraduate qualification in marketing	*ein Aufbaustudium in Marketing machen*
drive	*Energie; fahren*
executive	*leitender Angestellter*
experience	*Erfahrung*
fine print	*das Kleingedruckte*
fine touch	*Fingerspitzengefühl*
foul things up	*Mist bauen*
guideline	*Richtlinie*
immediately available	*sofort verfügbar*
interpersonal skills	*Fähigkeiten im zwischenmenschlichen Bereich*
light bulb	*Glühbirne*
main aims	*wichtige Ziele*
medical technology	*Medizintechnik*

merger	*Firmenzusammenschluss*
omnipotence	*Allmacht*
permit	*gestatten, erlauben*
physical lay-out of the room	*Raumgestaltung*
pick up	*verstehen*
pluck	*rupfen*
probe	*tasten, prüfen*
promote	*befördern; fördern*
propose	*vorschlagen*
purpose of a question	*Zweck einer Frage*
questionnaire	*Fragebogen*
relax	*sich entspannen*
require	*erfordern*
save	*retten; sparen*
sermon	*Predigt*
suggest	*vorschlagen, anregen*
turkey	*Truthahn*

Time for a smile

Dr Block wanted to promote one of his junior managers to the senior executive level. He handed out a questionnaire to the possible candidates. One of the questions was: "Do you believe that you have executive potential?"
One of the candidates wrote in answer: "I think I have executive potential because I like to be alone, I never get lonely, and I would like to work in a private office on my own, and I don't care if people say bad things about me."

3 Chapter

PREPARING THE BUSINESS TRIP*

Well, needless to say Dr Tissmann got the job. He was commissioned *from* the Board to go to MEDIMAKE in Nottingham, the land of Robin Hood and what's left of Sherwood Forest. His role was to be a torch-bearer, a bridge-builder. *Among others* he was to talk to key people, decision-making "little Englanders" to allay their fears etc. The buzzword was synergy. And time was short. It was June 1st and Tissmann had to be in Nottingham by June 15th. "Where's my secretary?"

At the travel agency

A Cork travel agent looked out through his window to see an old lady and an old man gazing longingly at his display of posters of exotic holiday resorts. As a publicity gimmick he decided to offer them a free round-the-world cruise with all expenses paid. When they returned some months later he asked the old lady if she had enjoyed herself. "*Wonderfully*," she replied, "but tell me one thing. Who was that old man I had to share my cabin with every night?"

ATTENTION, PLEASE!

There are four things to improve in the above text and in the dialogue. We've marked them in *italics*. Can you correct them?

---

* Mehr über *idioms* und *phrases* für die Reise in *Master your Business Phrases. Sprachmodule für den Geschäftsalltag*, rororo sprachen.

Preparing the flight

T: Mrs Sparkler, *here Tissmann.* I need your help. I'm planning to fly to Manchester Airport next week.
S: And how long will you be staying?
T: Well, indefinitely until I hear otherwise.
S: Exactly what date would you like to travel?
T: On the 7th June.
S: Okay. Shall I make a hotel reservation for you in Manchester?
T: No, we'll need to check out the situation in Nottingham. I *stay* there at least three months. Can you call me back when you've got the details?

TASK 1: Pitfalls for Germans

Here are four things for you to improve.

1. He was commissioned *from* the Board to go to MEDIMAKE in Nottingham.
2. *Among others* he was to talk to key people to allay their fears.
3. Mrs Sparkler, *here Tissmann.* I need your help.
4. *I stay* there at least three months.

Time for a smile

Shortly after the plane took off, the passengers heard a soft and comforting voice through the loudspeaker: "Welcome on board our completely automatic supersonic airliner. We are happy to have you with us. This plane is completely automatic: automatic pilot, automatic services, automatic starting and landing devices. Absolutely nothing can go wrong ... go wrong ... go wrong ..."

TASK 2: Build your phrases for flying the friendly skies

Ich möchte gerne einen Flug nach London buchen.	I'd ________ to book a flight to London.
Einfach oder hin und zurück?	Single or ______________?
Was kostet der Flug zurzeit?	What's ____ ____ of the flight at the moment?
Erste Klasse oder Touristenklasse?	Do you want to fly first class or __________ ?
Und wie sieht es mit dem Rückflug aus?	And ________ ________ the return flight?
Wann, sagten Sie, startet die Maschine?	When does the plane _________ off, did you say?
Ist das Ortszeit?	Is that _________ __________?
Ist es dort früher oder später als bei uns?	Are they _________ of us or behind us?
Ihr Anschlussflug ist um 14 Uhr.	Your ______________ flight is at 2.00 p.m.
Sie haben zwei Stunden Aufenthalt in Chicago.	You'll have a _______ _________ in Chicago.

Time for a smile

The managing director of a big multi-national company was persuaded against his will to take a trip round the world on Concorde. Having a very heavy workload he decided to take some files with him. As they were flying over Europe, the stewardess, in an attempt to make the trip entertaining, said, "That's Rome down there, sir." "Don't bother me with details," snapped the executive. "Just mention the continents."

Booking a room

The phone is ringing, a receptionist (**R**) answers.

S: Hello, my name's Sparkler. I'm phoning from Germany. I saw your hotel advertised in the Internet.
R: What facilities do you require, madam?
S: A single room with all the mod cons. And you have fax, e-mail and Internet, don't you?
R: Yes, and small meeting rooms, sauna, whirlpool, massage, whatever you want.
S: Dr Tissmann *is non-smoker.* Do you have rooms for people like that?
R: Of course.
S: And the price is still *actual* – as stated in the Internet?
R: Yes, Ma'am. Could you confirm your booking by fax, please?

How to keep travel expenses down

Traveller:	Excuse me, do you have a room for tonight?
Hotel owner:	Certainly, sir. It'll be fifteen pounds a night. Or I can let you have a room for only five pounds, if you make your own bed.
Traveller:	I'll take the five-pound room.
Hotel owner:	Right. I'll just go and fetch the wood, hammer and the nails for the bed.

TASK 3: More pitfalls for Germans

See also Task 5.

1. Dr Tissmann *is non-smoker.*
2. Yes, it's all *actual.* Could you confirm your booking by fax, please?

TASK 4: Build your phrases for a good night's rest

Ich möchte gern ein Zimmer reservieren.	I'd like to book a room, ________.
Wie lange möchten Sie bleiben?	How long _______ you like to _____?
Auf welchen Namen, bitte?	______ _______ name, please?
Einzel- oder Doppelzimmer?	_________ or ___________?
Was kostet das für eine Nacht?	________ _______ _______ that per night?
Ist das Frühstück inbegriffen?	Does that ____________ breakfast?
Leider muss ich meine Reservierung stornieren.	I'm afraid I have to __________ my booking.
Würden Sie das bitte per Fax bestätigen?	Would you ____________ that _______ fax, please?

TASK 5: Tricky words

One word in German – three words in English

aktuell für	*aktuelle Situationen* *den neuesten Stand* *aktuelles Interesse*	current up-to-date topical

actual(ly) =	*tatsächlich* *wirklich* *eigentlich*

Now it's your turn. Can you master these phrases?

A: The question of GM food is of _____________ interest. What is the Government's ___________ stand on biogenetics?

B: No need to worry, they say. _________ , scientists are not sure at all.

A: By the way, the list you gave me yesterday containing the test results of GM food is not _____________ .

B: I know, those were the glossed-over results from the producers. The _____________ results are in the pipeline.

TASK 6: Spot the mistake

There's one mistake in each sentence. Can you spot it?

1. I will fly to Manchester airport next week.
2. I phone from Germany. I want to book a room.
3. And how long do you stay?
4. I have seen your hotel advertised in the Internet.

Food for thought

Ronny told Annette that actually there was a chance that genetically manipulated food might hurt his reproductive organs. She said in her opinion it was a small price to pay.

FOCUS: Getting to know the public telephone

Instructions you will find on the telephone

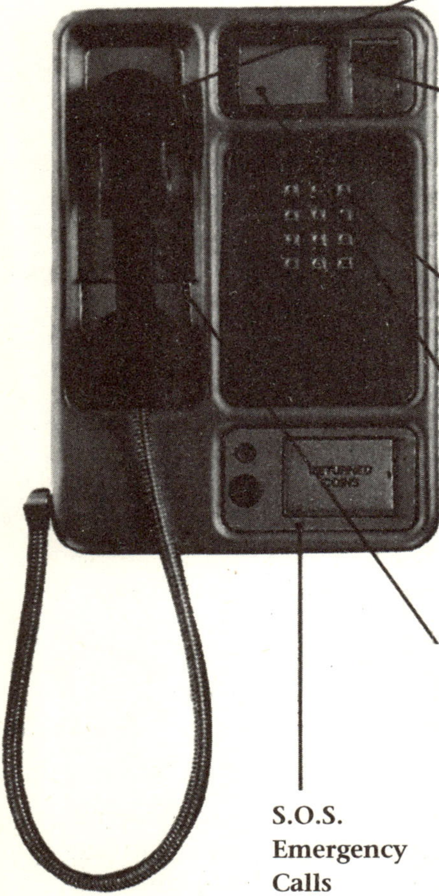

1. Lift handset
Hörer abnehmen

2. Insert money
Geld einwerfen

3. Dial Number
Nummer wählen

4. Follow on calls
Press button then redial
Weitere Gespräche – Knopf drücken und erneut wählen

5. Replace handset
Hörer einhängen

6. Unused coins returned
Rückgabe nicht benötigter Münzen

S.O.S.
Emergency
Calls
Notrufe
Polizei
Dial 999

A poster gives you the following information

Prices using coins	Gebühren im Münzbetrieb
Local calls: 67 seconds per 10p unit, equivalent to 9p per minute.	**Ortsgespräche:** 67 Sekunden für 10 Pence, entsprechend 9 Pence pro Minute.
UK long-distance calls: 43 seconds per 10p unit, equivalent to 14p per minute.	**Ferngespräche** innerhalb des Vereinigten Königreichs: 43 Sekunden für 10 Pence, entsprechend 14 Pence pro Minute.
Different rates apply to calls made by credit, debit BT charge card and calls made via the operator.	**Verschiedene Gebühren** für Gespräche mit BT-Kundenkarte und Gespräche über die Vermittlung.
International calls: calls to premium numbers and mobile phones may incur considerably higher charges.	**Auslandsgespräche:** Verbindungen zu Telefonsonderdiensten und Handys können erheblich teurer kommen.
Coins: only unused coins are returned. For short calls avoid using 50p or £1.	**Münzen:** Nur nicht benutzte Münzen werden zurückgegeben. Nehmen Sie für kurze Gespräche keine 50p- oder 1£-Münzen.

Time for a smile

McNab, a real Scotsman, decided to get married. So one morning he sent telegrams to three of his girlfriends proposing marriage. Two phoned to say 'yes' immediately, and the third phoned that night to say the same. He married the third girl saying, 'The girl for me is the one who waits for cheap rates at night.'

MAGIC squares

How would a native speaker react? Match stimulus and response. Put the right numbers in the magic squares below. All columns and rows will add up to the same number.

1. Here you are.	**2.** What can I do for you?	**3.** For five years.
4. How do you do?	**5.** Of course. Go ahead.	**6.** Since 1998.
7. You're welcome.	**8.** Fine. Thank you.	**9.** Yes, please.

A. How are you today?
B. Can I have your biro?
C. How long have you lived in Germany?
D. And how long did you live in Italy?
E. May I use your phone?
F. Thanks a lot.
G. How do you do?
H. Can I help you?
I. This is Tom Prox speaking.

A =	**B =**	**C =**
D =	**E =**	**F =**
G =	**H =**	**I =**

WORD AID

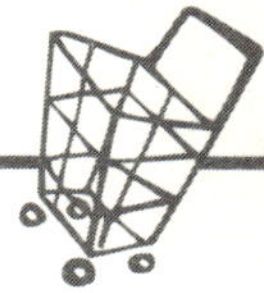

advertise	*annoncieren*
among other things	*unter anderem*
at least	*mindestens, wenigstens*
bridge-builder	*Brückenbauer*
buzz-word	*Reizwort, Modewort*
comforting	*beruhigend*
commissioned; be ~ by	*beauftragt sein von*
contain	*enthalten*
device	*Vorrichtung*
expenses	*Auslagen, Kosten*
facilities	*Ausstattung, Einrichtung*
file	*Akte*
night rates	*Nachttarife*
gaze longingly at ...	*sehnsüchtig blicken auf ...*
gloss over	*schönfärben*
holiday resort	*Ferienort*
in the pipeline	*in Bearbeitung*
indefinitely	*auf unbestimmte Zeit*
mention	*erwähnen*
mod cons (modern conveniences)	*moderner Komfort*
needless to say	*es bedarf keiner Erwähnung*
persuade someone	*jemanden überreden*
propose marriage	*einen Heiratsantrag machen*
publicity gimmick	*Werbetrick, -masche*
remove fears	*Befürchtungen zerstreuen*
reproductive organs	*Fortpflanzungsorgane*
require	*wünschen, fordern, benötigen*
snap	*aufbrausen*
stand	*Standpunkt*
state a price	*einen Preis angeben*
supersonic airliner	*Überschallpassagierflugzeug*
torch-bearer	*Vorreiter*
workload	*Arbeitslast*

4 Chapter

ARRIVING IN A FOREIGN COUNTRY

You would think that travelling across borders in Europe might be the easiest thing in the world – but don't believe a word of it. In many countries you still have to show your passport, the customs authorities still make spot checks, luggage disappears without the faintest trace and the traffic is more dangerous than ever.

Time for a smile

A German on a cruise on the Amazon is watching the native fishing boats on the huge river. Suddenly one of the boats capsizes and the three natives are howling desperately for help. Immediately some crocodiles approach them. "Typical!" the German exclaims. "Nothing to eat, but lifeboats from Lacoste!"

ATTENTION, PLEASE!

There are three things to improve in the dialogue. We've marked them in *italics*. Can you correct them?

Passport problem

A week later Tissmann (T) has collected his few rags and bags and stuffed his diary and schedule of meetings into a suitcase. The flight was okay. He landed in Manchester (centre of the football world) and went through passport control for passengers from non-European countries. An immigration officer (I) stops him.

I: Good afternoon, sir, could I see your passport, please?
T: Certainly, *please.*
I: Hmm! This is a German passport.
T: Anything wrong? *I'm member* of the European Union, you know.
I: Excuse me, sir, but this passport expires in the next four weeks. It's not really valid any longer. It could expire while you're still in the country. How long will you be staying here?
T: Well, I'm not sure. About three months, I guess. And I'll be *visiting* some conferences. Look, normally my ID card should be enough. I shouldn't really even show my passport.
I: Sorry sir. These are the rules here, and we all have to follow them. I'll let you through now, but I recommend you renew your passport immediately.

TASK 1: Keywords in Business

ein Pass ist abgelaufen	a passport has ________________
nicht mehr gültig sein	be no longer ________________
einen Pass erneuern lassen	______ one's passport ________
So sind die Vorschriften hier.	These are the ____________ here.

TASK 2: Could you correct the mistakes in the text?

1. Good afternoon, sir, could I see your passport, please? – Certainly, *please.*
2. I'll be *visiting* some conferences.
3. Anything wrong? *I'm member* of the European Union, you know.

(See also Tasks 4 and 5 for hints)

TASK 3: Talk your way through passport control

Put the words in the box into the dialogue.

plan renew purpose expire nationality stay use declare business (plus three prepositions of your choice)

Passport control	You
What's your _______________?	I'm German.
What's the ___________ of your visit?	I'm here _____ _______________ .
I'm afraid your passport has ____________.	Too bad! Can I _______ it ____________ _____ my consulate?
How long ______ you _________ to stay?	I' __ ____ _________ ___ a week.
Have you got anything to ______________?	No, I've only articles for my personal _____________ .

TASK 4: Tricky words

One word in German – two words in English

besuchen	Personen, Orte besuchen, inspizieren	**visit**
	1. Einrichtungen regelmäßig besuchen 2. teilnehmen an	**attend**

Most people in England *attend* school up to the age of sixteen.
Schools are *visited* regularly by school inspectors.

What not to say to the customs official

When Tom was crossing the border into Canada, they asked if he had any firearms with him. He said, "Well, what do you need?"

To complicate things a little, here are some more phrases to keep you in touch with people. Can you fit them into the following dialogue.

attend	**go to**	**go and see**	**see**	**pay a visit**	**visit**

Use each expression from the list only once. Sometimes you have to change the form of the verb. Good luck!

Boris Zuchov (**Z**), Receptionist (**R**)

Z: Good morning. I've an appointment to (1) _______________ my friend Block.

R: I'm afraid Dr. Block is not in. He's (2) _________________ a conference in Zurich. He will be back tomorrow.

Z: What about his son? Has he joined the company in the meantime?

R: No, Mr Zuchov. He still (3) _______________ university.

Z: Hmm. I might as well (4) _______________ to Mrs Block and her children. Could you give her a ring please?

R: I'm afraid she's in hospital. Would you like to (5) __________ her there?

Z: I'm not sure if she would like that. I think I'll (6) ______________an old friend of mine first. See you tomorrow.

TASK 5: More tricky words

One word in German – four phrases in English

bitte (sehr / schön) =	(yes,) please
	you're welcome
	go ahead
	here you are

How would you react?

Another cup of tea?	
May I use your phone?	
Have you got an aspirin for me?	
Thank you for helping me.	

Master your phrases: Entering a foreign country

At the passport control

Würden Sie bitte Ihre Landekarte ausfüllen?	Would you please fill in your landingcard?
Ihren Ausweis, bitte.	Could I see your passport please?
Ich fürchte, Ihr Pass ist abgelaufen.	I'm afraid your passport has expired.
Ich habe leider vergessen, ihn verlängern zu lassen.	I'm afraid I forgot to have my passport renewed.
Kann ich mit meinem Konsulat telefonieren?	Can I phone my consulate?
Ich habe leider kein Visum.	I'm afraid I haven't got a visa.
Könnten Sie mir eine Aufenthaltsgenehmigung ausstellen?	Could you issue me with a residence permit?
Was ist der Zweck Ihrer Reise?	What's the purpose of your visit?
Ich bin geschäftlich hier.	I'm here on business.
Ich besuche einen Geschäftsfreund in Tokio.	I'm going to visit a business friend in Tokyo.
Ich gehöre zu einer Reisegesellschaft. Unser Führer ist bei der Passkontrolle.	I belong to a party. Our guide is at passport control.
Wie lange haben Sie vor, zu bleiben?	How long will you be staying?
Ich bleibe eine Woche.	I'll be staying for a week.
Ich mache eine Rundreise.	I'm making a round trip.
Würden Sie bitte das Einwanderungsformular ausfüllen?	Would you please fill in the immigration form?

What not to say to the customs official

"Any alcohol?" demands the Saudi customs official.
"No, thanks," answered Klaus, "I've got enough in my suitcase."

At the customs

Haben Sie etwas zu verzollen?	Have you got anything to declare?
Ich habe nur Waren für meinen persönlichen Gebrauch.	I only have articles for my personal use.
Würden Sie bitte diesen Koffer öffnen?	Would you open this suitcase, please?
Was befindet sich in Ihrer Tasche?	What is in your bag?
Nur ein paar Geschenke und Souvenirs.	Only a few presents and souvenirs.
Entschuldigen Sie bitte. Muss ich diese Zigarren verzollen?	Excuse me, sir, do I have to pay duty on these cigars?
Haben Sie zollfreie Waren gekauft?	Did you buy anything tax free?
Wie viel ist zollfrei?	What's the duty-free allowance?
Für dieses Paket müssen Sie eine Zollerklärung ausfüllen.	You have to fill out a custom's declaration for this parcel.
Tut mir Leid, aber Parfum ist ein zollpflichtiger Artikel.	Sorry, but perfume is a dutiable item./ Sorry, but you have to pay duty on perfume.
Die 20 Uhren, die ich gekauft habe, sind immer noch in der Zollabfertigung.	The 20 watches I bought are still in customs clearance.

A stewardess remembers

A man tried to get on a British Airways flight with a little Yorkshire terrier in his arms. The stewardess told him that dogs were not allowed on board, so he went to the airport shop and bought himself a pair of dark glasses and a white walking-stick.
This time he was greeted by another stewardess who said, "It's quite unusual to see a Yorkshire terrier as a guide-dog, sir. They're usually Golden Labradors."
"You mean this isn't a Golden Labrador?" said the man in surprise.

Luggage trouble

Tissmann (T), having waited half an hour for his luggage, goes to the lost luggage office and speaks to the clerk (C).

C: Can I be of assistance, sir?
T: Well, I certainly hope so. I'*m waiting* for my luggage *since* more than half an hour. It simply hasn't arrived.
C: Not to worry. There's probably a good reason for it. What was your flight number?
T: BA 2715 from Frankfurt.
C: Yes, that plane has certainly landed.
T: Of course it has. I'm the living proof, aren't I? But my cases didn't turn up.
C: All the luggage from 2715 has passed through the system. Apparently there are still some suitcases that are unclaimed. Where exactly were you standing, sir?
T: Over there, at the Manchester reclaim. It's empty, as you can see.
C: Excuse me for saying so, sir, but that belt is for luggage from Stuttgart to Manchester. Your luggage return is at the other end of the hall.
T: Oh, my goodness! I only *remarked* the destination, Manchester. Sorry for all this trouble. Bye-bye (he rushes off).

ATTENTION, PLEASE!

There are three things to improve in the text and in the jokes below. We've marked them in *italics*. Can you correct them?

Boss: I hope you don't mind me saying this, but there's a lot of dust on my desk! It looks as if it hasn't been cleaned *since* months.
Cleaning lady: Don't blame me, sir. I have only been here for last week.

"I'm not my usual self tonight," Tom *noticed*.
"Yes, I've *remarked* the improvement."

TASK 6: Could you correct the mistakes in the text?

1. I'm waiting for my luggage since more than half an hour.
2. I only remarked the destination, Manchester.

Murphy's Law of flying

The distance to the gate is inversely proportional to the time available for catching your flight.
As soon as the stewardess serves the coffee, the airliner encounters turbulence.
When the plane you are on is late, the plane you want to transfer to is on time.
Whichever baggage claim you stand by, your baggage will come in another one.

Luggage problems

Wie komme ich zur Gepäckausgabe?	Where's the baggage claim, please?
Ich kann mein Gepäck nicht finden.	I can't find my luggage.
Mein Koffer war nicht dabei.	My case hasn't turned up.
Gehen Sie zum Fundbüro.	Go to Lost and Found / the Lost Property Office.
Jemand hat meinen Koffer vertauscht.	Someone has switched suitcases with me.
Mein Koffer ist beschädigt worden.	My suitcase has been damaged.
An wen kann ich mich wenden?	Where can I report it?

FOCUS: Setting foot on British *soil*

Boden

Working in the U.K.

If you have the luck to be a *citizen* of the EU you can work in Britain without a *permit*. Citizens from a Commonwealth country who are under 27 can work *part-time* for up to two years.

Bürger
Erlaubnis
halbtags

Documents

If you want to enter Britain you *need to have* a *valid* passport. If you're from the EU, US, Canada, New Zealand or Australia you don't need a visa. When you arrive at a British air or *seaport* you will find separate queues at *immigration control*. Don't *despair*! One is for EU people, the other lines are for everybody else. EU citizens can pass through a blue *channel*, everybody else should go through the customs channel.

haben müssen
gültig
Hafen
Einwanderungs-kontrolle
verzweifeln
Durchgang

Customs

Zoll

Go through the green channel if you have nothing to declare. But *beware*, there are still random checks for everybody! For "everybody else" there are still *restrictions* on alcohol: two litres of wine, plus one litre of alcoholic drink over 22 per cent vol., 200 cigarettes or 50 cigars. Don't try to bring your animals into Great Britain. They will be put into *quarantine* for several months.

Vorsicht
Beschränkung
Quarantäne

MAGIC Squares

Match the jokes with the words. Put the right number in the magic squares below. All columns and rows will add up to the same number.

Anders: *different* or *other*? **Art:** *art* or *kind* or *sort*?
Etwas: *something* or *anything*? **Hören:** *listen* or *hear*?

1. listen	**2.** hear	**3.** art
4. something	**5.** sort	**6.** anything
7. kind	**8.** other	**9.** different

A. Never invest your money in that eats or needs repairing.
B. A small thing can be made large by the right of advertising.
C. Jake went for a medical check-up. "Your ears are getting worse," said the Doc. " You will have to cut out drinking, smoking and sex." "What?" cried Jake in alarm, "just so I can better?"
D. If you want your wife to , then talk to another woman.
E. James Kelly is the of American who would call John the Baptist Jack.
F. He is an original player. He makes a lot of mistakes, but they are always each time.
G. "Do you know a man with one leg called Moloney?" – "No. What's the name of his leg?"
H. Architecture is the of how to waste space.
I. An intellectual is a man who has found more interesting than women.

A =	B =	C =
D =	E =	F =
G =	H =	I =

WORD AID

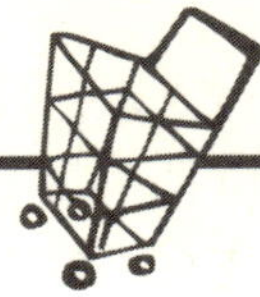

approach	*sich nähern*
available	*verfügbar*
capsize	*kentern*
cruise	*Kreuzfahrt*
customs authorities	*Zollbehörde*
cut out drinking	*das Trinken aufgeben*
exclaim	*ausrufen*
expire; a passport expires	*auslaufen*
facilities	*Einrichtungen*
firearms	*Feuerwaffen*
give someone a ring / bell	*jemanden anrufen*
guess	*annehmen, raten*
immigration officer	*Einwanderungsbeamter*
improvement	*Verbesserung*
John the Baptist	*Johannes der Täufer*
lifeboat	*Rettungsboot*
luggage return	*Gepäckrückgabe*
meantime; in the ~	*inzwischen*
mod cons (modern conveniences)	*voller Komfort*
not be valid any longer	*nicht mehr gültig sein*
rags; his few ~ and bags	*seine Siebensachen*
recommend	*empfehlen*
renew a passport	*einen Pass erneuern*
require	*erfordern, brauchen*
rule	*Regel, Vorschrift*
price is as stated	*Preis wie angegeben*
trace; without the faintest ~	*ohne die geringste Spur*
unclaimed suitcases	*nicht abgeholte Koffer*
valid	*gültig*

RENTING A CAR* Chapter 5

Dr Tissmann (T) wants to rent a car for two or three days until he's settled in. An English friend living in Germany advised him not to rent at the airport. "You'll pay the double at HEART OR RAVIS", he warned the dynamic doctor. Tissmann, always a good man to save a penny, decided to take a taxi to the nearest village. "I'm going to hire a car locally", he grunted. Ten minutes later and £10 lighter he opened the door of DAVE'S CARS FOR ALL (**D**) in Drearby near Manchester.

Let's start with a smile

On the motorway at night, a driver hears on the radio traffic service: "This is a warning. Watch out for a driver going in the wrong direction." The driver grumbles: "One driver? There are hundreds, hundreds of them."

ATTENTION, PLEASE!

There are five things to improve in the dialogue.
We've marked them in *italics*. Can you correct them?

* Siehe auch *Master Your Business Phrases. Sprachmodule für den Geschäftsalltag*, rororo sprachen.

Bureaucratic baggage

T: (banging a bell) Hi, anybody home?
D: (Dave shuffles in from the backroom) Hello. Can I help you? Be careful with that bell. It was a present.
T: Oh, excuse me.
D: What can I do for you, mate?
T: Well, I'd like to hire a car, please.
D: So you want to rent a car? That's what we're here for. What size of car do you want?
T: I'd prefer a comfortable car, with a manual gear change.
D: All our cars have gears of one sort or another. They introduced them about fifty years ago.
T: I mean I don't like automatic transmission.
D: Oh, I get you. You want a manual. Well, we've got a lovely Saab on the forecourt.
T: Saab? Hmmm! Well, it depends on the cost. I have a budget to keep to.
D: Oh, short of money!
T: Well, *I wouldn't say that exactly.*
D: What about that Ford over there? That's cheap enough.
T: Might be okay. How much is that per week?
D: Three hundred quid.
T: Three hundred pounds. That's a bit expensive.
D: No way! You've got unlimited mileage. Go as far as you want. The world's your oyster, as they say.
T: Is fully comprehensive insurance included in the price?
D: Well, no. Of course, that's different for every driver. Look at this form. You've got to fill that out and name the driver, presumably yourself. Just an extra fifty pounds.
T: Okay, I'll take the car and the personal insurance. How much is that?
D: Three hundred and fifty pounds for the week.
T: (Tissmann remembers that Heart was £85 cheaper, but it's too late now) Okay, let's do it! Do you take Master's Card?
D: Just a minute, mate. We've got a procedure to go through. May I have a look at your driving licence, please?

T: *Please.*

D: Jesus, what's this? It's written in foreign. I can't read that.

T: I must admit that it's my old licence. I haven't ...

D: (interrupting) Now, just a minute! We're in the European Union and there are standard driving licences. What's your permanent address?

T: *Kleinschmidtstraße 13* in 69115 Heidelberg.

D: I beg your pardon. Where's that?

T: It's in Baden-Württemberg in the south of Germany.

D: Bardewittybog, Jesus Christ. I'm sorry mate. I can't do it. I can't take a risk with you. God knows what sort of driving tests you have there. I'm sorry.

T: Oh, my God. You're not going to *make* business with me? This is impossible. This place is *behind the moon.* Goodbye.

Time for a smile

A Trabi makes your average Skoda
look like a Ferrari.

I once bought a car designed for five people:
one had to drive while the other four pushed.

TASK 1: Test your memory

1. Why doesn't Tissmann rent a car at the airport?
2. What kind of car is he looking for?
3. Why does Dave refuse to do business with Tissmann?

TASK 2: Keywords in business

ein Auto mieten	to __________ a car
ein Auto mit Schaltautomatik	a car with automatic ______________
Sie wünschen Gangschaltung?	You want a __________ gear change?
ein Budget einhalten müssen	have a budget to __________
knapp bei Kasse sein	be _____________ of money
es hängt vom Preis ab	it _____________ on the price
unbeschränkte Kilometerzahl	unlimited _____________
Vollkaskoversicherung	fully _____________ insurance
im Preis inbegriffen	_____________ in the price
ein Verfahren einhalten müssen	have a _____________ to go through
ein Formular ausfüllen	______ _______ a form
Wo ist Ihr ständiger Wohnsitz?	What's your _____________ address?

TASK 3: Pitfalls for Germans

1. I wouldn't *say that exactly.*
2. What's your permanent address? – *Kleinschmidtstraße 13*, 69115 Heidelberg
3. May I have a look at your driving licence, please? – *Please.*
4. You're not going to *make* business with me?
5. This place is *behind the moon.*

TASK 4: Beef up your word power

Say it another way.

Can I be of assistance?	Can I ______ _______?
I'd rather have a comfortable car.	I'd _________ a comfortable car.
I want to say I don't like automatic transmissions.	I _____________ I don't like automatic transmissions.

TASK 5: Joke your way round trouble spots

One word in German – two words in English

machen	**make**	betont das Ergebnis
	do	betont die Tätigkeit

1. "Waiter! Waiter! What (*macht*) this fly in my soup?" – "Hmm ... Looks like breast-stroke, doesn't it?"
2. "I've prepared the turkey," said Ronny to his girlfriend. "I've plucked it and stuffed it. All you've got to (*machen*) is kill it and cook it."
3. A hedgehog finding himself on top of a scrubbing brush: "We all (*machen*) mistakes, don't we?"

TASK 6: More about the trouble maker: *machen*

Choose a word from the box.

do go hold take

eine Prüfung machen	____________ an exam
Urlaub machen	____________ on holiday
Überstunden machen	____________ overtime
eine Geschäftsreise machen	____________ a business trip
jemanden verantwortlich machen	____________ someone responsible

If more than one person can (*verantwortlich machen*), nobody will be found to blame.

Last year we were on the edge of an abyss – This year we've (*machen*) a big step forward.

Master your phrases: Renting a car

Entschuldigen Sie, wo ist der nächste Autoverleih?	Excuse me, where is the nearest car rental, please?
Ich möchte gerne einen Wagen mieten.	I'd like to rent a car, please.
Wie lange brauchen Sie ihn?	How long do you want it for?
Ich möchte einen Wagen für heute mieten.	I'd like to hire a car for the day.
Wünschen Sie einen bestimmten Wagentyp?	Do you want a certain class, sir?
Wie groß soll der Wagen sein?	What size car do you want?
Mir genügt ein Mittelklassewagen.	A family car will do.
Wie viel kostet ein Ford Cortina pro Tag?	How much is the daily rental for a Ford Cortina?
Ich bin automatische Schaltung nicht gewöhnt.	I'm not used to automatic transmission / gearshift.
Ich hätte lieber einen Wagen mit Gangschaltung.	I'd prefer a car with a manual gear change.
Und wie viel macht das pro Woche?	How much is that per week?
Sind die Kilometer inbegriffen?	Is the mileage included?
Ja, Sie haben unbegrenzte Kilometerzahl.	Yes, you've unlimited mileage.
Ist Vollkaskoversicherung im Preis inbegriffen?	Is fully comprehensive insurance included in the price?
Unsere Autos sind haftpflichtversichert.	Our cars are insured for third party.
Was deckt die Versicherung ab?	What does the insurance cover?
Vollkasko müssen wir gesondert berechnen.	For comprehensive insurance we have to charge you extra.
Wie hoch ist die Selbstbeteiligung?	How much is the excess?
Wie hoch ist die Kaution?	How much is the deposit?
Darf ich bitte Ihren Führerschein sehen?	May I have a look at your driving licence, please?
Könnten Sie mir bitte Ihren ständigen Wohnsitz nennen?	Could I have your permanent address?
Bitte unterschreiben Sie hier.	Please sign here.

Diese Kopie ist für Sie.	That's your copy.
Und hier sind Ihre Schlüssel.	And here are your keys.
Kann ich eine Straßenkarte haben?	Could I have a road map, please?
Das Auto steht auf dem Parkplatz.	The car is in the car park.
Der Wagen wird vor dem Flugplatz stehen.	The car will be waiting outside the airport.
Was mache ich, wenn ich eine Panne habe?	What do I do in case of a break-down?
Wo kann ich das Auto in Glasgow zurückgeben?	Where can I return the car in Glasgow?

TASK 7: Rent your car

1. I'm not used to automatic ___________
2. I'd prefer a car with a ___________ ___________
3. What does the insurance ___________?
4. Is fully ___________ insurance ___________ in the price?
5. How much is the daily ___________ for a Ford Cortina?
6. Where can I ___________ the car in Glasgow?

Time for a smile

Why does a Lada have a heated rear-windscreen?
To keep your hands warm when you push it.

MAGIC squares

Match the jokes with the words. Put the right number in the magic squares below. All columns and rows will add up to the same number.

1. newest	**2.** most	**3.** least
4. normal	**5.** common	**6.** ordinary
7. latest	**8.** the most	**9.** last

A. Experts at the Pentagon were scratching their heads about what to do next. Their most complicated code had been cracked by teenagers using ___ computers.

B. The ___ kind of computer was presented at the Cebit. Somebody asked it, "What will Germany be like in 2020?" The answer came back in Chinese.

C. One girl told her friend, "He not only lied to me about his yacht, but I had to do ___ of the rowing."

D. My ___ invention is an automatic pancake. You put popcorn in the dough so that it will turn over by itself.

E. Of the six senses, the most important is ___ sense.

F. A husband's ___ words are always, "Okay, buy it."

G. Selling is ___ exciting thing you can do with your clothes on.

H. People who can ___ afford to pay rent. pay rent. People who can most afford to pay rent, build up equity. MURPHY'S LAW

I. "Movie cowboys mystify me", said the actor Bob Hope. "How can they jump off a porch roof and onto a horse, and still sing in a ___ voice?"

A =	B =	C =
D =	E =	F =
G =	H =	I =

FOCUS: A bit about business in Britain

You can do business in the United Kingdom by *establishing* a *representative office* or a *subsidiary*. A subsidiary must *adopt* one of the country's existing legal forms. And here they are:

einrichten
Vertretung, Tochtergesellschaft; annehmen

Private limited company (Ltd.)

- There must be at least one *shareholder.*
- The minimum capital *required* is two shares for at least £2.
- Shareholders' *liability* is limited to the capital invested.
- There may be at least one director.

Anteilseigner
erforderlich
Haftung

Public limited company (PLC)

- Must have at least two shareholders.
- Fully *subscribed capital* of at least £50,000, one quarter must be *paid up.*
- Operates like a private limited company, but has a *board of directors.*
- Shareholders' *liability* is limited to the capital invested.

Stammkapital, Einlage; einzahlen
Vorstand
Haftung

Partnership

- Has no corporate personality or status.
- Needs at least two partners and no more than 20.
- Partners are *liable jointly* for all *debts.*

Gesellschaft des bürgerlichen Rechts; gemeinsam haftend; Schulden

What about the poor worker or clerk? What does his contract *contain*? If you have a *permanent* contract it will be in written form signed by the employer and the employee. It will contain:

enthalten; unbegrenzt

Length of the working week

The legal maximum is 48 hours. Most categories of worker have between 35 hours and 45 hours. It depends on the *terms* of the *collective bargaining agreement.*

Bedingungen; Tarifvertrag

Overtime

This varies, but in general 100% *premium* is paid for overtime on Sundays and during paid holidays.

Überstunden
Prämie

Annual vacation

Two to four weeks a year, *depending on* contract, age and *length of service.*

abhängig von
Betriebszugehörigkeit

Wages

There is a *statutory minimum wage.* There may also be additional *benefits*: bonuses, *profit-sharing,* private medical cover etc.

gesetzlicher Mindestlohn; Zulagen
Gewinnbeteiligung

These are only a taste of the employment conditions. That was the good news. The bad news is that you must pay taxes, too. Never mind! There is often a good atmosphere at work.

Time for a smile

I once worked for a company where they had a bonus system. After six months they told me that I owed the company money.

WORD AID

abyss	*Abgrund*
admit	*zugeben*
bell	*Glocke*
bonus system	*Prämiensystem*
breast-stroke	*Brustschwimmen*
common sense	*gesunder Menschenverstand*
comprehensive insurance	*Vollkaskoversicherung*
designed for five people	*für fünf Personen ausgelegt*
dough	*Teig*
driving licence	*Führerschein*
equity	*Eigenkapital*
fill out a form	*ein Formular ausfüllen*
forecourt	*Hof*
grumble	*murmeln*
grunt	*grunzen*
have a budget to keep to	*ein Budget einhalten müssen*
heated	*beheizt*
hedgehog	*Igel*
locally; hire a car ~	*ein Auto vor Ort mieten*
manual	*Schaltgetriebe*
mate	*Kumpel*
normal	*(physisch, geistig) normal*
ordinary	*gewöhnlich, handelsüblich*
owe money	*Geld schulden*
pancake	*Pfannkuchen*
personal insurance	*Haftpflicht*
presumably	*vermutlich*
procedure	*Verfahren, Vorgehensweise*
push	*schieben*
quid (pound)	*Pfund*
rear-windscreen	*Heckscheibe*
scratch one's head	*sich am Kopf kratzen*
scrubbing brush	*Schrubber*
settle in	*sich eingewöhnen*
turkey	*Truthahn*
unlimited mileage	*unbegrenzte Kilometerleistung*

6 Chapter FIRST CONTACT WITH THE NATIVES

It's a typical situation to arrive in a foreign country and get stressed because the traffic is complicated, the streets are busy – the whole system is different. Tissmann was stressed, and then the last straw, the hotel syndrome.

Time for a smile

A man walked up to the desk of a hotel and asked for a room.
"Have you a reservation?" asked the indifferent clerk.
"No. But I've been coming here every year for twelve years, and I've never needed a reservation."
"Well, there is nothing available. We are fully booked, and without a reservation you can't get a room."
"Suppose the President of the United States came in. You would have a room for him, wouldn't you?"
"Of course, for the President we would find a room."
"Alright," said the man. "Well, the President isn't coming here tonight. So give me his room."

ATTENTION, PLEASE!

There are five things to improve in the dialogue. We've marked them in *italics*. Can you correct them?

Traffic problems and hotel trouble

Dr Tissmann (T) eventually reaches the airport and rents a car with no further problems. He drives down to Nottingham, but can't find the hotel. He pulls the car over to the side of the road and engages a policeman (P) in conversation.

T: Excuse me, officer, I seem to be lost. I'm looking for a hotel, The Victoria. Can you show it me on this *card?*
P: Now sir, what card are you talking about? Oh, I see. You've got a street map. Well, before we go into directions it's my duty to inform you that you're travelling in the wrong direction up a one-way street.
T: Oh, my goodness! Sorry, sir. I'm *not used to drive* in such a big city as Nottingham.
P: Well, see that you turn your vehicle around and go back down the street. Now, where do you want to go? The Victoria. Yes, you're a stone's throw from it. Drive back down here, first right to the traffic island and go off the island at three o'clock. And it's on the corner.
T: Three o'clock? Why should I wait for an hour?
P: I beg your pardon? Three o'clock? I mean the island is a clock face. Take the exit which is located at three o'clock.
T: Got it! Thank you. Goodbye!

Of course, there was more confusion. Tissmann had some problems driving on the left and with a right-hand drive car. Somewhat stressed he arrived at the Victoria Hotel. The receptionist (R) greets him.

R: Good afternoon. Can I be of help?
T: Yes, I hope so. My name's Tissmann. I believe a room has been reserved for me.
R: Tissmann? How do you spell that, please?
T: Oh, T, E, SS, M A N N.
R: Tessmann. I ...
T: Sorry, I've got it wrong. I meant to say TISS – Tissmann.
R: Well, it doesn't help. There is no room reserved for you here and we're fully booked. There's a conference on. I can recommend a small hotel nearby.

T: Now, just a minute. I really want to complain about the service here. I'm going to *control* the information in my fax from you. After all, there's a lot of *concurrence* in your business and my company will *eventually* use your service very often. I'm sure it's rare that you have a visitor staying for two months.

R: Sir, we do our best to please. Two months, did you say? There is a reservation for a Mr Mediquip, but that doesn't sound much like Tissmann.

T: That's it! I work at MEDIQUIP.

R: Right. So that's solved. Here are the keys. Do you need a porter?

T: It's safer if I do it myself. Goodbye!

One hour later a red-faced Tissmann arrives at the reception desk.

T: Excuse me, I'm in room 206. I'd like to see the manager. I have a complaint to make.

C: Oh dear. I'm sorry to hear that. What exactly is the problem?

T: First of all, I can't flush the toilet. It doesn't work. And by the way the tap drips. I can't afford not to sleep. Look here, I have your advertisement here. What you describe is ...

C: If I could break in a moment, sir, of course it'll be our pleasure to relocate you to another room. Perhaps on the rear side of the hotel where it's quieter. I'll arrange for your things to be moved.

T: All right. Well, thank you very much.

C: Sorry for any inconvenience caused.

A hotel you should avoid

Notice in an Egyptian hotel:
The water in this establishment is completely hygienic.
It has all been passed by the manager.

TASK 1: Key words in business

ein Zimmer reservieren	______________ a room
ausgebucht sein	be ______________ booked
ein Hotel empfehlen	______________ a hotel
bei einer Firma arbeiten	work ______ a company
eine Reklamation haben	have a ______________ to make
sich über den Service beschweren	____________ about the service
einen Gast in einem anderen Zimmer unterbringen	__________ a guest to another room
Entschuldigen Sie die Unannehmlichkeiten.	Sorry for any ____________ caused.

TASK 2: Pitfalls for Germans

(See also Task 5 and 6)

1. The Victoria. Can you show it me on this *card*?
2. I'm *not used to drive* in such a big city as Nottingham.
3. I'm going to *control* the information in my fax from you.
4. After all, there's a lot of *concurrence* in your business and my company will *eventually* use your service very often.

TASK 3: Test your memory

1. What did the policeman tell Tissmann before he showed him the way?
2. Why was there no room booked for Tissmann?
3. Why was Tissmann relocated to another room?

In case of trouble get an efficient lawyer

My lawyer's beyond brilliant. In a recent case some of you may have read about, he told his client: "Don't worry. The judge is my cousin. Their chief witness goes with my secretary. And I'm planning to bribe four of the jurors. Meanwhile, try to escape!"

TASK 4: Beef up your word power

Say it another way. Find the synonym.

So that's *settled.* There is a *booking* for a Mr M. We'll *move* you to another room. If I *may interrupt* you, sir.	So that's ______________ . There is a _____________ for a Mr M. We'll ______________ you to another room. If I ________ __________ ____, sir.

TASK 5: Joke your way round trouble spots

One word in German – three words in English

Karte	card
	map
	ticket

1. Without a _________ you'll lose your way on your trip to Hudson Bay.
2. You buy a _________ to watch cricket.
3. Tom signs his _________ with 'kind regards'.

Another nonsense rhyme so that you won't confuse English *map* with German *Mappe, Aktentasche:*

4. A manager without his __________ is in the office out of place.

TASK 6: More tricky words

kontrollieren	**is not always**	control

It's your turn again.

1. Tissmann's passport was ___________ by the immigration officer.
2. He was going to ___________the information in the fax from the hotel.
3. A policeman was ___________ the traffic at the traffic island.
4. Why is it that this company cannot ___________ its cashflow?

And another pitfall for Dr Tissmann:

Eventuell	**is not**	eventual(ly)

1. He *(endlich)* reached the airport.
2. He had a street map in order to avoid *(eventuelle)* traffic jams.
3. My company will *(vielleicht)* use your service very often.

PHRASES Master your phrases: Accommodation matters

Hotel services

Liegt eine Nachricht für mich vor?	Are there any messages for me?
Könnten Sie meine Wertsachen in den Safe tun?	Could you please put my valuables in your safe?
Können Sie mein Gepäck auf das Zimmer bringen lassen?	Could you have my luggage sent up / taken up to my room?
Kann ich meine Kleider reinigen lassen?	Is there a laundry service?
Wann wird Frühstück serviert?	When is breakfast served, please?
Ich bräuchte ein Ferngespräch nach München.	I need a long-distance call to Munich.
Können wir in unserem Zimmer frühstücken?	Could we have breakfast in our room?
Wir wollen nicht gestört werden.	We don't want to be disturbed.

How to complain

Ich würde gerne den Geschäftsführer sprechen. Ich habe eine Reklamation.	I'd like to see the manager. I've a complaint to make.
Ich möchte mich über den Service in Ihrem Hotel beschweren.	I want to make a complaint about the service at your hotel.
Ich möchte mich beschweren.	I've got a complaint to make.
Der Wasserhahn tropft.	The tap drips.
Ich hätte gerne ein anderes Zimmer.	Could I have a different room, please?
Die Toilettenspülung funktioniert nicht.	The lavatory won't flush.

Checking out

Ich reise morgen ab. Könnten Sie bitte meine Rechnung fertig machen?	I'm leaving tomorrow. Could you get my bill ready?
Ich hätte gerne eine getrennte Rechnung für meine Telefongespräche.	Could I have a separate bill for my telephone calls, please?
Führen Sie bitte alle Posten einzeln auf.	Can you let me have an itemised bill, please?
Schicken Sie die Rechnung bitte an Dolittle Ltd., Bristol.	Please send the bill to Dolittle Ltd in Bristol.
Kann ich meinen Koffer für ein paar Stunden unterstellen?	Could I leave my suitcase here for a couple of hours?
Wecken Sie mich bitte um 7 Uhr. Ich muss meinen Zug erreichen.	Could you please wake me at 7a.m. I've a train to catch.
Könnten Sie mir ein Lunchpaket mitgeben?	Could I have packed lunch, please?
Würden Sie mir bitte ein Taxi für sieben Uhr morgens bestellen?	Would you please order a taxi for me for seven o'clock?

Time for a smile

The pretty bell girl of the Hilton in Boston showed Renny Bosy to his room. Renny asked her what the rates were. "Eighty dollars," said the girl. "That's reasonable," said Renny, "I'll pay the eighty dollars with pleasure ..." – "With pleasure," interrupted the girl, "it'll be five hundred."

TASK 7: Let's test your memory

1. I've a *(Reservierung auf den Namen Meier)*.
2. Is there any *(Nachricht für)* me?
3. Do you want *(Vollpension)* or only *(Frühstück)*?
4. I'd like to *(sprechen)* the manager. I've got a *(Reklamation)* to make.
5. Could you *(meine Rechnung fertig machen)*?
6. Could I have a *(getrennte Rechnung)* for the calls?

TASK 8: A mixed bag of questions

1. What do you put into the hotel safe?	your ....
2. Another word for booking:	....
3. What's the document called you have to fill in?	....
4. Three meals at the hotel:	....
5. They clean and iron your clothes:	....
6. If you are not satisfied, you make a	....
7. You want a detailed bill. Ask for an	.... bill

Surprise at the check out

Robert went to check out of his London hotel and asked for his bill. "We hope you enjoyed your stay," said the receptionist. Robert, looking at the bill: "Yes, I did, but I think I should have stayed much longer, since I've practically bought the place."

MAGIC squares

Match the sentences with the words. Put the right number in the magic squares below. All columns and rows will add up to the same number.

bemerken: *realise, notice* or *remark?*
leihen: *lend* or *borrow?*
glücklich: *happy* or *lucky?*
(er)sparen: *spare* or *save?*

1. saved	2. borrow	3. happy
4. realised	5. remarked	6. lend
7. noticed	8. lucky	9. spared

A. Fred is ___. He has a wife and a transistor, and they both work.
B. A consultant is someone who has ___ his client almost enough to pay his fee.
C. A bank is a place that will ___ you money if you can prove that you don't need it.
D. Best wishes for a ___ and successful first marriage.
E. Jones was reading his paper. "That's terrible! Statisticians have found out that every time I breathe out a man dies." – "Then it's high time," ___ Smith, "that you bought a mouthwash."
F. "I'm not myself today." – "Yes, I've ___ the improvement."
G. Did you hear about the policeman who gave out a hundred parking tickets before he ___ he was at a drive-in movie?
H. If Columbus hadn't discovered America, he would have ___ us a lot of trouble.
I. If you want to know the value of money, go and try to ___ some.

A =	B =	C =
D =	E =	F =
G =	H =	I =

WORD AID

bell girl / boy	*Hotelpage*
borrow something	*sich etwas leihen*
break in	*unterbrechen*
breathe out	*ausatmen*
bribe	*bestechen*
complain	*sich beschweren*
complaint	*Beschwerde, Reklamation*
directions	*Erklärungen, Anweisungen*
eventually	*schließlich*
flush the toilet	*die Toilette spülen*
improvement	*Verbesserung*
inconvenience	*Unannehmlichkeit*
indifferent	*gleichgültig*
juror	*Geschworene(r)*
knee bends	*Kniebeugen*
lend	*verleihen*
mouthwash	*Mundwasser*
parking ticket	*Strafzettel*
pass something	*absegnen, prüfen*
pass water	*Wasser lassen*
rate	*Tarif, Preis*
rear side	*Rückseite*
recent; a ~ case	*ein kürzlicher Fall*
recommend	*empfehlen*
relocate someone to another room	*jemandem ein anderes Zimmer geben*
sign in	*sich eintragen*
straw; the last ~ that breaks the camel's back	*der letzte Tropfen, der das Fass zum Überlaufen bringt*
suppose	*annehmen, gesetzt den Fall*
value	*Wert*
witness	*Zeuge*

7 Chapter BUYING THINGS

In the UK the opening times of shops are more flexible than in Germany and times of closing are not standardised. It depends where you buy. Our hero had his first experiences of this in Nottingham, a city located in the Midlands of England. He still has to learn to 'chill out'.

Murphy's Law about buying clothes

1. If you like it, they don't have it in your size.
2. If you like it and it's in your size, it doesn't fit anyway.
3. If you like it and it fits, you can't afford it.
4. If it fits, it's ugly.
5. If you like it, it fits and you can afford it, it falls apart the first time you wear it.

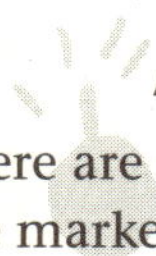

ATTENTION, PLEASE!

There are six things to improve in the dialogue.
We've marked them in *italics*. Can you correct them?

Running around the shops

It's 6 p.m. and Dr Tissmann (T) has to go to the shops. He's unpacked his suitcase and has noticed that he's forgotten several things. He rushes out. "Oh dear, what a stress! The shops will be closed." However, a pleasant surprise – a clothes' shop on the corner is open. The shopkeeper (S) welcomes him, smelling some business.

T: Hello. I think I've just made it. Oh dear, I'm *sweated through*.
S: Take it easy, mister. Chill out a bit. Sit down! There's no hurry.
T: Thank God. When do you shut?
S: We're open till 8 p.m. On Saturdays we close a little earlier.
T: So late? I had no idea. Well, that's great! Listen, I need socks. I *let my suitcase pack* by my secretary. And that's it! All wrong.
S: Do it yourself if you want it done well, I always say. What's your size?
T: Forty-three or forty-four, I think.
S: Oh, I see. That'll be an eight and a half. Look at these colours, feel the material. You'll go a long way till you find something like that. It's a real bargain.
T: I'm sure you're right. I'll take them. And I need a pair of shoes ...

Half an hour later Tissmann arrives at W.H. Smoth, a famous, if not serious, bookshop.

T: Good evening, I'm looking for a book.
S: Well, I certainly hope so, sir, otherwise you wouldn't be here, would you? Ha, ha, ha.
T: Hmm. Glad you find it all so funny. Well, at least I have enough time.
S: Sorry, sir. We close at seven. You've got five minutes.
T: Five minutes? Well, perhaps you can help me. I want a ... *Roman*.
S: Ha, ha, ha! I want one too, as long as she's female.
T: I beg your pardon. I'm referring to a book. Two hundred pages, fiction.
S: Oh, I get you. You're looking for a novel. What about? A detective, an adventure story?
T: A novel and adventure, but with a background in *technic*.
S: If you'll come with me. We've got something for you. Isaac Asimov. Science fiction.

Dr Tissmann is a passionate eater .
So he pops into the local corner shop.

S: How can I help you, my dear?
T: I was looking for some fruit. *Have you eventual some* pineapples and mangos?
S: Oh, I'm sorry, my love. I don't stock that exotic stuff. No call for it. I could do some nice apples and pears for you.
T: Okay, I'll take two of each.
S: And something special just for you. Look! Lovely sumptuous Victoria plums. Bet you've never seen the likes of them before. Try one, me duck.
T: Hmmm! They are delicious. I'll have a kilo.
S: How many, my sweet?
T: Oh, two pounds.
S: Here you are.
T: Can I pay with a card?
S: Oh dear, my love. I'm a cash only shop. What would I be wanting with cards?
T: Okay. No problem. There's a *money automat in the near of* my hotel. No problem.
S: Well, dear me. What's a money automat?
T: Never mind! It's a long story.

TASK 1: Key words in business

Wir *haben* bis 20 Uhr geöffnet.	We __________ open till 8 p.m.
Wir *schließen* um 19 Uhr.	We ___________ at 7 p.m.
Welche Größe haben Sie?	__________ your _____________ ?
Fühlen Sie einmal das Material.	_____________ the material!
Ich *führe* diese Waren nicht.	I don't __________ these goods.
Wir verkaufen *nur gegen bar.*	I'm a _________ __________ shop.
Das ist ein *Schnäppchen*.	It's a ____________ ____________ .
Geld aus dem *Automaten* holen	get money from a _____ _________
keine *Nachfrage nach* Mangos	no __________ ______ mangos

TASK 2: Pitfalls for Germans

Could you correct these mistakes? (See also tasks 5 and 6)

1. I'm *sweated through.*
2. I *let my suitcase* pack by my secretary.
3. I want a ... *Roman.*
4. A novel with a background in *technic.*
5. *Have you eventual some* pineapples?
6. There's a *money automat in the near of* my hotel.

TASK 3: Test your memory

1. Tissmann needs size 43 socks. What size should he ask for in Britain?
2. Where in the world do you find Romans and novels?
3. What do money and weight have in common in Britain?

TASK 4: Beef up your word power

Say it another way. Find a synonym.

What can I do for you?	How ______ ______ ______ _____ ?
What size do you take?	What's __________ __________?
I'm talking about a book.	I'm ______________ _____ a book.
You've never seen anything like those before.	You've never seen the __________ of __________ before.
I'll take a kilo.	I'll __________ a kilo.
Do you accept cards?	Can I ________ ________ a card?

TASK 5: Joke your way around trouble spots

One word in German – three words in English

schließen	shut
	close
	lock

Which word fits best?

1. Modern architecture: "In my experience, if you have to keep the lavatory door ______________ by extending your left leg, it's modern architecture.
2. Etiquette is knowing how to yawn with your mouth ______________ .
3. Two business partners went fishing one Sunday together. As they were waiting for a nibble one suddenly exclaimed, "I think I forgot to ________________ the office safe!"
   "Don't worry," said his partner, "after all, we're both here."
4. I went down the street to the 24-hour grocery. When I got there, the guy was _______________ the front door. I said, "Hey, why are you ______________ ? The sign says you're open 24 hours." He said, "Yes, but not in a row."

TASK 6: More trouble spots to joke around

One word in German – four phrases in English

lassen	leave
	get, have done
	let do

1. Mother: Ronny's teacher says he ought to have an encyclopaedia.
   Father: Nonsense, ________________ him walk to school like I did.
2. The boss demanded to know where he had been.
   "I've been for a haircut."
   "You can't ________________ your hair cut in office time."
   "Why not? It grows in office time."
   "Not all of it," said the boss.
   "So I didn't ________________ it all cut off," he replied.
3. Father: How was your first day in school?
   Boy: Well. I'd hoped for more. I can't read. I can't write, and the teacher won't even ________________ me talk.
4. Advice to directors: Just ________________ the most difficult problems for the laziest managers to solve. They will come up with the quickest solutions.

PHRASES Master your phrases: Shopping English

Buying things

Guten Morgen. Werden Sie schon bedient?	Good morning. Are you being served?
Könnten Sie mir vielleicht helfen?	I wonder if you could help me.
Ich suche	I'm looking for ...
Die Strickjacke gefällt mir. Kann ich sie anprobieren?	I like this cardigan. Could I try it on?
Was für eine Größe tragen Sie?	What size do you take?
Ich habe Größe 52.	I take a size 42.
Diese Strickjacke ist leider zu eng an den Schultern.	I'm afraid the cardigan is too narrow across the shoulders.
Versuchen Sie es mit Größe 54.	Try a size 44.
Gibt es diese Strickjacke in anderen Farben?	Is this cardigan available in other colours?
Wie wäre es mit Gelb?	What about something in yellow?
Ich hätte gerne ein paar Schuhe, Größe 42.	I'd like a pair of shoes, size 8.
Sehen Sie diesen Regenmantel hier? Das ist wirklich ein Schnäppchen.	Look at this raincoat. It's a real bargain.

Time for a smile

After a tiring day's shopping, the perfect purchase is either in the first or the last shop you went into.

Paying for things

Wie viel macht das alles zusammen?	How much is that altogether?
Nehmen Sie Euros?	Do you accept Euros?
Ich möchte mit Kreditkarte zahlen.	I'd like to pay by credit card.
Wir können leider nur Barzahlung akzeptieren.	I'm afraid we are a cash only shop.
Wir benötigen eine Anzahlung von 10 %. Sie bezahlen den Rest bei Lieferung.	We require a deposit of 10 %. You can pay the rest on delivery.
Können Sie es bitte als Geschenk einpacken?	Could you gift-wrap it, please?
Könnten Sie es bitte an diese Adresse schicken?	Could you send it to this address please?

Good bargains

A bargain is something you buy that is cheaper than something you really want or need.

FOCUS: Shopping in Britain

Shopping across Britain is very *varied* and includes supermarkets, craft studios, farm shops, street markets and factory showrooms. Britain is well-known for its *country clothing,* wool and tweed etc.

verschieden

Kleidung im Lodenlook

When can you shop?

You will find shops open from 9 a.m. to 6 or 7 p.m. with many shops opening on Saturday and Sunday, so there is no stress. You can buy clothes rather cheaply in Britain (not in the centre of London, of course). Getting the *size* right is a problem. Here's a table to help you.

Größe

Get your size right

Shoes	UK	4	5	6	7	8	9	10
	Europe	37	38	39	41	42	43	44
Men's shirts	UK	15		15 1/2	16		16 1/2	17
	Europe	38		39	41		42	43
Men's suits	UK	38		40		42		44
	Europe	48		50		52		54
Blouses and dresses	UK	10		12		14		16
	Europe	38		40		42		44

Checking out

But when you choose something, please do not put it into your bag before you have been to the *till* (cash desk) to pay for it. It may be *presumed* that you are trying to steal it.

The *unpleasant* part is paying for something. The currency in England is the pound sterling. We have 1p, 2p, 5p, 20p, 50p, £1 and £2 *coins*. The notes are £5, £10, £20 and £50. In Scotland they *issue* their own notes. These can also be used in Britain.

zur Kasse gehen
Kasse
annehmen, vermuten
unangenehm
Münze
ausgeben

Paying

For those of you who *consider* notes & coins to be old-fashioned, you can use VISA, Masters or Access cards. *Beware!* Few shops will accept cheques *drawn on* foreign banks.

If you find yourself without food and drink in the evening, search out the nearest *"off-licence"*. These places are open late, normally managed by Pakistanis or Indians, because some modern English people are too lazy to work in the evenings. You can buy beer and wine, bread, vegetables and anything you want. Most of them even have a large *selection* of videos nowadays.

halten für
Vorsicht!
ausgestellt auf
Tante-Emma-Laden
Auswahl

MAGIC squares

Match the sentences with the words. Put the right number in the magic squares below. All columns and rows will add up to the same number.

- **Aktion:** is it *action, activity* or *campaign*?
- **blamabel:** is not *blamable*. Is it *blameworthy* or *embarrassing*?
- When is a man a *chef* and when a *boss*?
- What is the difference between *economic* and *economical*?

1. campaign	**2.** economic	**3.** action
4. blameworthy	**5.** chef	**6.** activities
7. boss	**8.** economical	**9.** embarrassing

A. Her ___ include tennis and painting.
B. Who's the ___ in this house?
C. It is not always ___ for buses to run on Sundays.
D. The company ran a successful advertising ___ to promote its new brand of washing powder.
E. The Waldorf Astoria is very satisfied with its new ___.
F. He suffered an ___ defeat.
G. Larger tubes of toothpaste are more ___.
H. Let's put this plan into ___.
I. It was a ___ mistake to make.

A =	B =	C =
D =	E =	F =
G =	H =	I =

Double check the Magic squares

sparsam:	______________________
Aktion:	______________________
blamabel:	______________________
Chef:	______________________
wirtschaftlich:	______________________

WORD AID

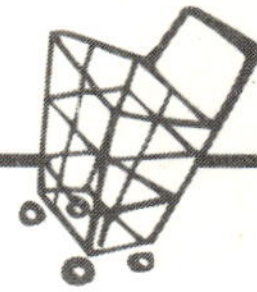

chill out	*relaxen, sich entspannen*
defeat	*Niederlage*
delicious	*köstlich*
disgraceful; it's ~	*es ist eine Schande*
eventual(ly)	*schließlich*
extend	*ausstrecken*
fall apart	*zerfallen, auseinander fallen*
fiction	*Belletristik, Literatur*
in a row	*durchgehend; hintereinander*
knee bends	*Kniebeugen*
lavatory	*Toilette*
nibble	*Biss (beim Angeln)*
novel	*Roman*
pineapple	*Ananas*
purchase	*Kauf; kaufen*
rush out	*hinauseilen*
shut	*schließen; zumachen*
size	*Größe*
sumptuous	*prächtig, üppig (Mahl)*
ugly	*hässlich*
yawn	*gähnen*

Time for a smile

Lady Wilberforce rang for the hotel manager who came up immediately. "I've a complaint to make," she said, "In the room opposite there's a man doing knee bends – completely naked. It's disgraceful!" The manager looked out of the window. "Excuse me, but I'm afraid I can only see his head," he said. "Well," said the lady angrily, "you just stand on this chair."

8 Chapter VISITING BUSINESS PARTNERS

Cross-cultural behaviour is all the rage nowadays. It's really important to get to know the habits of your business partners and their countries. For example, in some societies you can arrive late for appointments, in some you can discuss business at lunch, while others prefer a sober and business-like atmosphere. Our Uwe, for example, is not yet familiar with the "over-relaxed" British ways. Read on!

Some like it "not"

A breakfast meeting is the most uncivilised idea I've ever heard of. If you're going to have a breakfast meeting, it should be in bed with a beautiful woman.
Gordon White

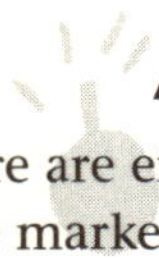

ATTENTION, PLEASE!

There are eight things to improve in the dialogue.
We've marked them in *italics*. Can you correct them?

Arranging an appointment

Dr Tissmann has had a couple of days to settle in. The next stage is to make first contacts with the key people at MEDIMAKE. He has a list of the big wigs. He phones the secretary of one of them.

S: Hello, Julia Watts speaking. How can I help you?
T: Hello, Dr Uwe Tissmann from MEDIQUIP in Germany *on the phone*. Could I *talk* to John Gaylor, please? Is he *there*?
S: I'll just see if he's in. Who shall I say is calling, sir?
T: I thought I told you. Tissmann. Uwe Tissmann.
S: Sorry, sir. Didn't catch it first time. Mr Gaylor will speak to you now. Putting you through.
T: Hello, Mr Gaylor?
G: Yes, John Gaylor. That's me. What can I do for you?
T: I'm from MEDIQUIP. The name's Tissmann.
G: Ah yes, we've been expecting you. When can you get in to see me?
T: Oh, it's *equal*. When do you have time?
G: Let's make it this afternoon, shall we?
T: Fine. I'm looking forward to *see you*.

First encounters

Mr Gaylor's office is on the 16th floor. Dr Tissmann knocks on the open door. Gaylor is already waiting.

G: Hi, John Gaylor. And you must be Dr Tissmann. Just call me John.
T: *Uwe Tissmann. How do you do*?
G: Fine thanks. Say, why don't we have a chat in a more informal atmosphere. Look, I don't need to be in the office any longer today. What about going to the pub on the corner to chill out?
T: Oh, I had thought we would *talk about business.* I must get to know your department's processes.
G: I know, I know. That's no problem. I'll bring a few charts with me and we can discuss matters there.
T: As you like.
G: This way. By the way, did you have a good trip over?
T: The service on the plane wasn't too good, and I had problems with my luggage ...

In the Bull's Head

G: It's my round. What'll you have?
T: *I'll drink a fruit juice.*
G: Come on, try a drop of something stronger.
T: Okay, a coffee for me.
G: Well, I was thinking of a drop of whisky. Won't you join me?
T: Right. Good idea.
(Five minutes later)
G: ... so, as I was saying, our firm was founded in 1970 and our head office is still in Nottingham. I think we've survived because we're constantly innovating our product range. We do a lot of business in the UK, but we've been trying to break into Europe.
T: Yes, I think the European market can be quite *rentable*. What strategies are you following for the European market?
G: Well, I was hoping you might be able to tell me more.
T: Right. Well, it's true that we have taken a controlling interest. We're in the same field. And we've got parallel products. You know as well as I do what that can mean ...

TASK 1: Keywords in business

Kontakte mit Leuten in Schlüsselpositionen anbahnen	make __________ with __________ people
übers Geschäft reden	talk __________
Angelegenheiten besprechen	discuss __________
die Firma wurde 1970 gegründet	the firm was __________ in 1970.
die Produktpalette erneuern	________ the product _______
in den europäischen Markt eindringen	__________ __________ the European market
Strategien und Ziele verfolgen	__________ strategies and ________
die Kontrollmehrheit übernehmen	take a __________ interest
auf demselben Gebiet tätig sein	be in the same __________

TASK 2: Pitfalls for Germans

Could you correct these mistakes?

A. Cultural mistakes

1. *Uwe Tissmann*. How do you do?
2. Hello, *Dr Uwe Tissmann* from MEDIQUIP in Germany *on the phone*.

B. Idiomatic mistakes

3. I (had) thought we would talk *about business*.
4. *I'll drink* a fruit juice.
5. Could I *talk* to John Gaylor, please? Is he *there*?

C. False friend

6. Oh, it's *equal*. When do you have time?
7. I think the European market can be quite *rentable*.

D. Grammar

8. Fine. I'm looking forward to *see* you.

TASK 3: Test your memory

Do you remember how they ...?

offered assistance	How ____________ you?
	What ____________ you?
asked for a caller's name	Who ____________, sir?
said they didn't understand	I didn't ____________ it first time.
connected a caller	____________ you ____________.
suggested a meeting time	____________ this afternoon, shall we?
suggested a meeting point	____________ to a pub?

Time for a smile

The manager called his assistant in the office and closed the door sternly. "Now listen to me", he said. "There's £50 missing from the petty cash box. There are only two keys to that box. I have one and you have the other." – "Well", said the assistant, "suppose we each put in £25 and say no more about it!"

TASK 4: Joke your way round trouble spots

One word in German – three words in English

sagen	say
	tell
	speak

1. Judge: What ________ your husband _______ when you smashed up the new car?
   Wife: Am I to repeat the swear words?
   Judge: Of course not!
   Wife: He ____________ a word.

2. A diplomat is a man who can (*Ihnen sagen*) to go to hell in such a way that you actually look forward to the trip.

3. "You look worried. What _________ the doctor ________?"
   "He (*er hat mir gesagt, ich soll*) take these pills for the rest of my life."
   "So, what's the problem?"
   "He only gave me half a dozen."

4. How can I _________ that you are _______________ the truth?
   It takes two to _______ the truth – one to ______ and one to hear.

5. Today I dialled a wrong number. The other person, ___________, "Hello" and I ___________, "Hello, could I ________ to Joey?"
   He _________, "Ugh ... I don't think so ... he's only two months old."
   I _________, "_________ him that I'll wait."

Time for a smile

She answered the phone to hear a very repentant voice. "I'm sorry darling," he said. "I have thought it over and decided that you can have the Rolls as a wedding present and we will move to the Gold Coast immediately, and, okay, your mother can come with us. Will you marry me?"
"Of course I will," she said, "who's speaking?"

PHRASES

Master your phrases: On the phone

1. Answering the phone

Ruver Ltd. Guten Tag. Kann ich Ihnen helfen?	Ruver Ltd. Hello. Can I be of help?
Guten Tag. Was kann ich für Sie tun?	Hello. How can I help you?
Was kann ich für Sie tun?	What can I do for you?
Wen wünschen Sie zu sprechen?	Who would you like to speak to?

Telephone problems

When you dial the wrong number, you never get a busy signal.

2. Tell them who you are

Hier ist Jack Brown. Guten Morgen.	Jack Brown here. Good morning.
Hier spricht Tom Smith von der Firma Ruver.	This is Tom Smith of Ruver speaking.
Spreche ich mit Herrn/Frau ...?	Hello? Is that Mr/Ms ...?

Telephone problems

A caller who dials the wrong number will call a second time as soon as you have returned to your living room and made yourself comfortable.

3. Identifying the caller

Dürfte ich um Ihren Namen bitten?	Could I ask your name, please?
Wen darf ich bitte melden?	Who shall I say is calling?
Mit wem spreche ich, bitte?	Could I ask who I'm speaking to?
Entschuldigen Sie, wie, sagten Sie, ist Ihr Name?	I beg your pardon, what did you say your name was?

Spreche ich mit S.A.T. Bonn?	Am I speaking to S.A.T. in Bonn?
Herr Brain ... von welcher Firma, bitte?	Mr Brain ... which company are you from?

Telephone problems

I got an answering machine for my phone. Now when I'm not at home and somebody calls me up, they hear a recording of a busy signal.

4. Asking to be put through

Geben Sie mir bitte Ihre Verkaufsabteilung.	Could you put me through to your sales department, please?
Ich würde gerne Herrn B. sprechen, wenn das möglich ist.	I'd like to speak to Mr B. if it's possible.
Wäre es möglich, mit Frau Child zu sprechen, falls sie da ist?	Could I possibly speak to Ms Child, if she's in?
Ob Sie mich wohl mit Herrn Smith verbinden könnten?	I wonder if you could put me through to Mr Smith.

Telephone problems

I got up one morning and couldn't find my socks, so I called Information. She said, "Information. Can I help you?" I said, "I can't find my socks." She said, "They're behind the couch." And they were!

5. Asking what it's about

Würden Sie mir bitte den Grund Ihres Anrufs nennen?	Would you mind telling me what you are calling about?
Darf ich nach dem Grund Ihres Anrufs fragen?	May I ask the purpose / reason for your call?
Darf ich fragen, um was es geht?	May I ask what it is concerned with?
Und was betrifft es, bitte?	And what's it about, please?

6. Putting the caller through

Ich stelle Sie durch.	I'm putting you through.
Bleiben Sie am Apparat. Sie werden verbunden!	Hold the line. You are being connected now.
Augenblick. Ich stelle Sie durch.	Just a moment please. Putting you through.
Ich versuche Sie zu verbinden. Bleiben Sie bitte am Apparat.	Trying to connect you. Hold the line, please.
Tut mir Leid, ich kann ihn nicht erreichen.	Sorry, I can't get through to his *number.*

Telephone problems

The telephone will ring when you are outside the door, fumbling for your keys.

The telephone will ring when you are having a shower. You will reach it just in time to hear the click of the caller hanging up.

TASK 5: Typical mistakes on the phone!

Please correct!

1. Who do you like you to speak?
2. Could I ask who I am talking to?
3. I'm sorry, sir. I haven't quite caught your name.
4. Am I talking to ROBOTALOT in Bonn?

Master your phrases: Arranging appointments

1. Making an appointment

Ich möchte einen Termin mit Herrn / Frau ... vereinbaren.	I'd like to make an appointment with Mr / Ms ....
Wann würde es Ihnen passen?	When would it be convenient?
Welcher Tag passt Ihnen am besten?	What day would suit you best?
Wie wäre es mit Kalenderwoche 14?	How about week 14?
Das passt mir gut.	That suits me fine.
Können wir eine Uhrzeit ausmachen?	Can we agree on a time?
Sagen wir, sieben Uhr.	Let's say seven o'clock.
Sieben Uhr, wenn Ihnen das recht ist.	Seven o'clock. If that's all right with you.

2. Arranging the meeting point

Was halten Sie davon, uns in meinem Hotel zu treffen?	What about if we meet at my hotel?
Schlagen Sie den Treffpunkt vor.	You suggest the place.
Ich schlage vor, wir treffen uns am Bahnhof.	I suggest we meet at the station.
Warum treffen wir uns nicht bei mir zu Hause?	Why don't we meet at my home / place?
Treffen wir uns (doch) in Ihrem Golfclub.	Let's meet at your golf club.

3. Rearranging appointments

Ich fürchte, Dienstag geht bei mir nicht.	I'm afraid I can't make it on Tuesday.
Ich habe bis 3 Uhr zu tun.	I'm not free before 3 o'clock.
Leider bin ich schon ausgebucht.	Sorry, I'm already booked.
Ist es möglich, dass wir uns später treffen?	Is there any chance of us meeting later?

Vielleicht könnten wir uns heute Abend zu einem späteren Zeitpunkt treffen.	Well, perhaps we can arrange to meet later tonight.
Ich muss das Treffen leider absagen.	I'm afraid I'll have to call off / cancel the meeting.
Können wir den Termin auf nächste Woche verschieben?	Can we postpone the appointment until next week?
Könnten wir es eventuell auf Montag vorziehen?	Could we bring it forward to Monday, perhaps?

TASK 6: Making an appointment

1. I was wondering if we could possibly (*uns treffen*) next week.
2. What day would (*passen*) you best?
3. (*Sagen*) we Tuesday?
4. Would you like us to arrange (*Unterkunft*) for you?

TASK 7: Arranging place and time

Choose the correct verb form.

1. *I'm calling / call to* check the time of Monday's meeting.
2. How long are *you thinking / do you think* we'll need?
3. So, *we're meeting / we meet* at my hotel on the 12th of March.
4. I look forward to *seeing / see* you on the 12th.

Praising a manager

It was an executive dinner party. The director got up and tapped his glass:
"Today we honour a man who doesn't know the meaning of fear, a man who doesn't know the meaning of defeat or surrender. So we have all chipped in and bought him a dictionary."

FOCUS: How business partners see each other

The human brain loves to generalise, that is why we cannot *resist* generalising about national characters although we know that not all Englishmen are cold-blooded and that most Americans are not as *blunt* as John Wayne.

A *market research* firm, the Parkland Research Europe, carried out an *opinion poll* among 185 business executives, lawyers, engineers, teachers and other professional people from seven European countries. They published their *findings* in the Guide to National Practices in Western Europe. Here is a summary of what other nations thought of the Germans and the British.

Let us take the British first. The reactions were mixed. Some found them calm, stiff, reserved, open-minded and *trustworthy*. Others think they are *hidebound* and superior. Everyone was *unanimous* that they had an excellent sense of humour. The British themselves most *admired* the characters of the Dutch.

What about the Germans? Most Europeans agreed that the Germans had a high proportion of good qualities. And the Germans, of course, liked themselves best of all nations. They considered themselves tolerant, but nobody else did. They saw themselves as fashionable. Others found them *square*. The Italians were *dumbfounded* by the German capacity to get things done without *bribing* anyone, but regarded them as *utterly lacking in style*. The French regard the Germans with *suspicion* and a measure of *loathing*, and seek to *contain* them by *chumming-up*. To the Austrians a good German would be one who is far away – preferably across the Atlantic, or even further if they didn't depend on the Euros of the German tourists that *prevent* their economy from collapsing.

widerstehen
direkt
Marktforschung
Meinungsumfrage
Ergebnisse
vertrauenswürdig; borniert; einstimmig
bewundern
altmodisch
verblüfft
bestechen
äußerst stillos
Argwohn; Abscheu; im Zaum halten; anfreunden
verhindern

The English have always had a *high regard* for German cleverness and *thoroughness*, somehow imagining that of all Europeans, the Germans are most like themselves. This illusion probably has its *roots* in the fact that so many Germans have *occupied* the British throne or been powers behind it.
The Germans regard the English as being very nice and mostly harmless, almost German. They respect the Swiss for their *seriousness*, honesty, punctuality and *cleanliness* – and they have never been to war with the Swiss. However, they like the Americans best. For the Germans, the United States is the *headmaster* in the school of nations.

Hochachtung
Gründlichkeit
Wurzel
einnehmen
Ernst
Sauberkeit
Schulleiter

More in S. Zeidenitz, B.Barkow, *The Xenophobe's Guide to The Germans*. Ravette Publishing

A joke for the road

A businessman visiting Brighton stopped at a hotel for an early evening drink. In the bar he got to know a very attractive girl. After a few drinks he took her over to the reception desk and booked a double room for the night, signing in as Mr and Mrs Doorbar. The next morning after breakfast he was presented with a bill for £950. "What's all this?" he exclaimed. "I've only been here one night, haven't I?"
"You're quite right, Mr Doorbar," said the clerk, "but your wife has been here for a week."

MAGIC squares

Match the sentences with the words. Put the right number in the magic squares below. All columns and rows will add up to the same number, 15.

1. fabrication	**2.** deposit	**3.** bail
4. manufacture	**5.** expert opinion	**6.** caution
7. form	**8.** expertise	**9.** formula

A. They have considerable ___ in dealing with oil spills.
B. The newspaper story turned out to be a complete ___.
C. Such products should be treated with extreme ___.
D. He was set free on ___ of 100,000 dollars.
E. Before we buy this van Gogh, we'll commission an ___.
F. Please complete and sign the insurance claim ___.
G. Our firm is engaged in the ___ of plastics.
H. To calculate the area of a circle use the ___ $\pi \times 2r$.
I. I had to pay a £500 ___ to the landlord.

A =	B =	C =
D =	E =	F =
G =	H =	I =

Double check

Deutsch	Englisch	Deutsch	Englisch
Kaution (Gericht)		Kaution (Bank)	
Erfindung		Fabrikation	
Formel		Formular	
Expertise		Wissen	

Merke: caution = Vorsicht

WORD AID

WORD AID

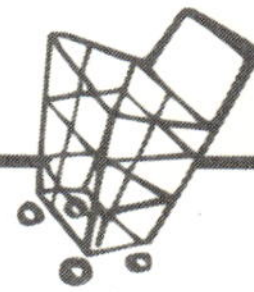

accountant	*Buchhalter*
answering machine	*Anrufbeantworter*
area	*hier: Fläche*
behaviour	*Verhalten, Benehmen*
big wig	*hohes Tier*
busy signal	*Besetztzeichen*
chat	*Plausch*
chip in	*(Geld) zusammenlegen*
cross-cultural	*kulturübergreifend*
defeat	*Niederlage*
fabrication	*Erfindung*
familiar with	*vertraut mit*
insurance claim	*Versicherungsanspruch*
oil spill	*Ölteppich, Ölunfall*
petty cash box	*Portokasse*
putting you through	*Sie werden verbunden*
rage; be the ~	*der letzte Schrei sein*
recording	*Aufzeichnung, Aufnahme*
rentable	*zu mieten*
repentant; a ~ voice	*eine reumütige Stimme*
smash up a car	*ein Auto zu Schrott fahren*
sober	*nüchtern*
sternly	*ernst*
suppose	*annehmen*
surrender	*Aufgabe; sich ergeben*
survive	*überleben*
swear word	*Fluch*

9 Chapter

A SPEECH OF INTENTION*

Uwe Tissmann has been at MEDIMAKE for more than three weeks getting to know the company. He's got a bit of an idea how things go on at MEDIMAKE and thinks it's about time he met the executives all together to clear up any doubts, rumours and misunderstandings. Tradition has it that every August there is a light-hearted conference for the middle level and top executives of the company which takes place in the banquet hall of Nottingham Castle. Tissmann decides to speak on this occasion.

Time for a smile

A speaker had just finished what he thought was one of his best after-dinner speeches when a drunk went over to him and said, "That was the most boring speech I have ever heard in my life." The chairman who hadn't heard what he had said dragged the speaker away and said, "Sorry about old Tomkins. But pay no attention to what he says. When he's drunk he only repeats what everybody else is saying."

ATTENTION, PLEASE!

There are five things to improve in the speech.
We've marked them in *italics*. Can you correct them?

Smoothing over fears

James Clondyke, Director of Sales, introduces Tissmann.

Ladies and Gentlemen, could I have your attention for a moment? Thank you. Well, as always the repast was more than delicious. Our host and the "Castle" have exceeded all our expectations again. I'm sure I speak for all of us when I offer you our heartiest thanks.
Today there is a slightly different turn of events. As you all know MEDIMAKE is involved at this moment in a merger with MEDIQUIP of Germany. Of course, this will include restructuring which will certainly affect many of us. In this regard there are fears here at the company, and naturally rumours. Rumours can get around like the flu and do no more good than that disease.
Today, Ladies and Gentlemen, maybe we have a doctor with us to cure the sickness. I am, of course, referring to our esteemed visitor today, Dr Uwe Tissmann, from our partner in Germany. Uwe, if I may introduce you informally, the floor is yours.

Uwe Tissmann puts down his glass and rises.

Thank you James, and thank you to you all for a really splendid dinner and an extra thank-you for your pleasant and relaxed company.
Colleagues, I want to be *short*. First, please forgive me for my English. Ten years ago I was better, but my present level *leaves a lot to wish*.
I am here to build bridges to our partners. I have a task, and this task can only be performed with your help. I am to check what products are produced, what markets we are in, what turnovers are made, and what the work processes are. *In the most cases* we all, or you all have nothing to fear. It can be that here or there jobs must be cancelled. But this *mustn't* mean *firings*. There are other ways.
Coming together in a merger of this kind is not the easiest thing to do. We must identify parallel work and complicated processes for the success of the company as a whole. And my hope and wish is that we do this together. To our co-operation!

TASK 1: Key words in business

Dürfte ich um Ihre Aufmerksamkeit bitten?	Could I ______________________, please?
Sie haben das Wort.	The ____________ is yours.
Missverständnisse aufklären	_________ ___ misunderstandings
jemandes Hoffnungen übertreffen	_________ someone's expectations
vor einer Firmenfusion stehen	be ____________ in a merger
Brücken zu seinen Partnern bauen	______ ________ to one's partners
eine Aufgabe erledigen	____________ a task
prüfen, welche Umsätze erzielt werden	____________ what ____________ are made

TASK 2: Pitfalls for Germans

Could you correct these mistakes?
(See also Tasks 5 and 6)

1. Colleagues, I want to be *short.*
2. In *the most cases* we all have nothing to fear.
3. But this *mustn't* mean *firings*.
4. My present level leaves a lot *to wish.*

How to thank the host

Thank you for that kind introduction. It seems that I shall now have to say two prayers for forgiveness: the first for my host for telling so many lies in praising me; the second for myself – for enjoying it so much.

TASK 3: Test your memory

1. What rumours or misunderstandings does Tissmann have to clear up?
2. How does he describe his mission at MEDIMAKE?
3. What is the task lying ahead of both companies?

TASK 4: Beef up your word power

False friend out! Tick it off ✔!

- ❑ takeover
- ❑ merger
- ❑ fusion
- ❑ joint venture

Now put the words next to their definitions.

1. ______________ : a project between two or more companies
2. ______________ : combining of two commercial companies into one
3. ______________ : melting different things together into one
4. ______________ : taking control of a company by buying most of its shares

TASK 5: Joke your way round trouble spot 'must'

nicht tun **müssen**
nicht tun **dürfen**
nicht zu tun **brauchen**

1. Two salesman met again after a night of hard drinking. "We (*nicht dürfen*) drink that much again," said Jones to Smith. "Do you remember that last night you sold Tower Bridge?"
   "Is that all?"
   "No, I bought it."
2. It's the final proof of God's omnipotence that he (*nicht brauchen*) exist in order to save us. PETER DE VRIES
3. An Italian prime minister (*nicht dürfen*) think of getting married until he gets a steady job.
4. Looking out of their tent, James and John saw a lion. The lion was coming nearer. James put his trainers on. "Why are you doing that?" John asked, "You are not faster than the lion!" – "I (*nicht müssen*) be faster than the lion," replied James, "I only (*nicht dürfen*) be slower than you!"
5. A German business man entered a Swiss bank. He looked carefully around, went to the reception desk and whispered, "I want to invest 300,000 marks." – "You (*nicht brauchen*) whisper," said the bank clerk, "poverty is nothing to be ashamed of."

TASK 6: Have a joke with 'most'

der, die, das meiste	*höchster Grad*: mehr als alle anderen, mehr als je zuvor	the most
am meisten	*hoher Grad*: fast alle(s), der größte Teil, die Mehrheit	most

1. When I was young I thought money was ________________ important thing in life. Now that I am old I know that it is. *Oscar Wilde*
2. ________________ women are not as young as they are painted.
3. Doctor: Say 'aaaaaah.'
   Girl: That's a change! ________________ young men want me to say 'yes'.
4. Selling is ________________ exciting thing you can do with your clothes on. *John Fenton*
5. One girl told her friend, "He not only lied to me about his yacht, but I had to do ________________ of the rowing."
6. A breakfast meeting is ________________ uncivilised idea I've ever heard of. If you're going to have a breakfast meeting, it should be in bed with a beautiful woman. *Gordon White*
7. Suicide is ________________ sincere form of self-criticism.
8. Ronald: Doctor, doctor my hands are trembling all the time.
   Doctor: I think you have got an alcohol problem.
   Ronald: Yes, doctor, I spill ________________ of it.
9. Just leave ________________ difficult problems for the laziest managers to solve. They will come up with the quickest solutions.
10. People who can least afford to pay rent, pay rent. People who can ________________ afford to pay rent, build up equity. *Murphy's Law*

Master your phrases: Making a speech

1. Introducing the speaker

Im Namen unserer Firma heiße ich Sie alle willkommen, um ...	On behalf of our company I'd like to welcome you all here to ...
Es ist mir eine große Freude, Ihnen Herrn X vorstellen zu dürfen.	I take great pleasure in introducing Mr X.
Wir haben die Ehre, Herrn X aus Y zum Thema Umweltbelastung zu hören.	We have the honour of being addressed by Mr X from Y on the topic of pollution.
Wir freuen uns alle auf Ihre Präsentation.	We're all looking forward to your presentation.
Mr X wird nun zu Ihnen über das Problem ... sprechen.	Mr X will now speak to you about the problem of ...

Introducing the speaker

My purpose is not to bore you, but to introduce people who will.

2. Introduce yourself

Ich bin Otto Daimler von der Firma MEDIQUIP *in Germany.*	I'm Otto Daimler from MEDIQUIP in Germany.
Ich war drei Jahre als Berater für ... tätig.	I was a consultant to ... for three years.
Ich kenne Ihre Probleme, da ich wie die meisten von Ihnen Verkaufs-manager gewesen bin.	I know your problems since I was a sales manager like most of you.
Ich bin auf diesem Gebiet auch nicht mehr Fachmann als Sie.	I'm no more expert in this field than you are.

How to introduce yourself

Before I get to the work at hand, let me say that to be chosen as your presenter is more than an honour. We had to draw lots to see who would be the presenter. I lost!

3. Creating a friendly atmosphere

Ich freue mich, dass ich die Gelegenheit habe, zu Ihnen über ... zu sprechen.	I'm glad to have the chance to speak to you on the subject of ...
Vielen Dank, dass Sie mich zum Thema ... eingeladen haben.	Thank you for asking me to tell you about ...
Ich bin Ihnen dankbar, dass Sie eine Stunde Ihrer wertvollen Zeit opfern, um mir zuzuhören.	I appreciate that you're sacrificing one hour of your valuable time to listen to me.
Ich bin dankbar, dass man mir Gelegenheit gibt, einige Missverständnisse aufzuklären.	I'm grateful for having been offered the opportunity to clear up some misunderstandings.

Creating a friendly atmosphere

I see we've got a very polite audience here tonight – they cover their mouths when they yawn.

4. Proposing a toast

Auf das Wohl der Firma!	To the company!
Ich schlage vor, wir trinken auf den Abschluss unseres Vertrags.	I'd like to propose a toast to the conclusion of our contract.
Erheben wir unsere Gläser und trinken auf die Zukunft Europas.	Let's raise our glasses to the future of Europe.
Ich erhebe mich, um auf das Wohl unserer Gäste zu trinken.	I rise to toast our guests.
Ich möchte einen Toast auf unseren neuen Kollegen ausbringen.	I'd like to propose a toast to our new colleague.
Meine Damen und Herren, begießen wir es mit einem Glas Champagner.	Ladies and Gentlemen, let's celebrate this with a glass of champagne.
Auf das Wohl der schönen Braut.	Here's to the beautiful bride.

TASK 7: Odd phrase out

Which phrase has a different meaning? Why?

I'm glad	that you're sacrificing one hour of your valuable time to listen to me.
I appreciate	
I'm grateful	

TASK 8: Let's woggle a few speech functions

Replace the *woggles* with a suitable word.

1. Ladies and Gentlemen, could I have your *woggle* for a moment?
2. I'm not going to *woggle* your valuable time. I want to be *woggle*.
3. I'm grateful for having been offered the opportunity to *woggle* up some *woggles*.

TASK 9: More tricky words

Stand up, rise and raise – which is which?

1. I ____________________ to toast the prosperity of our companies.
2. Let's ____________________ our glasses to the future of MEDIMAKE and MEDIQUIP.
3. Advice to speakers: ____________________ , speak up, shut up.

What to say to the audience

I'm delighted to see that you all have managed to come to this evening; you obviously didn't know that I was going to be making a speech.

FOCUS: Speaking to persuade

One of the most outstanding examples of a *contemporary* person who *has achieved success* because of his speaking *skills* is Lee Iacocca, the former CEO of the Chrysler Corporation. He used his talent as a speaker to win the *backing* of the President, Congress, and the American public in the largest corporate *bailout* in America's history. Even Iacocca credits his success to his skills as a speaker. In his autobiography, he writes: "I've seen a lot of guys who are smarter than I am and a lot who know more about cars. And yet I've left most of them in the smoke. Why? Because I'm *tough*? No. You've got to know how to talk to people, plain and simple."

All *persuasive* speakers have these things in common:

- They provide information so that the audience knows what to do.
- They try to overcome the listeners' *objections.*
- They appeal to emotions and *trust.*
- They *move* the listener to action.

And while speaking they all know that their success depends only up to 10 or 20 per cent on what they have to say. The rest is *voice* and body language. And they know that in this type of speech their argumentation has to be based on accurate logic. Nothing is more *destructive* than errors in logic.

These are the biggest mistakes you should *avoid:*

- *Oversimplification*
- *Begging the question*
- Misleading statistics
- *Obvious* manipulation

zeitgenössisch
erfolgreich sein
Fähigkeiten
Unterstützung
Firmenrettung
zäh, hart
überzeugend
Einwände
Vertrauen
bewegen, drängen
Stimme
vernichtend
vermeiden
Vereinfachung
am Thema vorbeireden; offensichtlich

Memorising a speech: The Five-Finger Formula

The Five-Finger Formula can help you to write and memorise your speech. Move each finger when you come to the next part of your speech.

Little finger	1. Catch the listeners' attention
	2. Tell them what you are going to talk about
Ring finger	1. Describe the problem or the situation
	2. Give examples
Middle finger	1. Weaken the counter-arguments, the strongest first, the weakest last.
	2. Present your arguments or your solution. Weak arguments first, strong arguments last.
Forefinger	1. Show the advantages
	2. Present examples and supporting evidence
Thumb	1. Summarise your arguments
	2. Ask them to take action
	3. Thank them for their attention.

Checklist for persuaders

1. Research how other people feel about your topic.
2. Select the most effective arguments.
3. Present your weak arguments first, your strong ones last.
4. Weaken the strongest counter-argument first, the weakest last.
5. Supply your arguments with good examples, facts and figures.
6. Take into account possible objections from the audience.
7. Restate your arguments at the end.
8. Paint the future bright.
9. Appeal for action.
10. Don't ever lose sight of what you want them to do.

Great lies told at meetings

This'll be a short meeting.
I'll only talk for about five minutes.
To cut a long story short ...

MAGIC squares

Match the sentences with the words. Put the right number in the magic squares below. All columns and rows will add up to the same number.

1. deficient	**2.** defect	**3.** stationery
4. client	**5.** definite	**6.** definitive
7. defective	**8.** stationary	**9.** customer

A. "I'd have to be an idiot to buy stock in your company," said the ✋. "OK. How many shares do you want?" replied the broker.

B. Have you ever eaten in a Paris restaurant? The real waiters are the ✋.

C. The Elk test has revealed a mechanical ✋ in the Mercedes A Klasse.

D. Tom lost his job because he stole ✋ from the company.

E. I want a ✋ answer, 'yes' or 'no'.

F. New test methods have shown that the engine of the car was ✋.

G. My wife crashed into a ✋ vehicle.

H. Our knowledge of the universe is still extraordinarily ✋.

I. Einstein's theory may not be the ✋ explanation of the universe.

A =	**B =**	**C =**
D =	**E =**	**F =**
G =	**H =**	**I =**

Double check

Deutsch	Englisch	Deutsch	Englisch
defekt		*definitiv, fest*	
Defekt		*endgültig*	
unvollkommen		*Büromaterial*	

WORD AID

WORD AID

affect someone	*jemanden betreffen, tangieren*
afford; be able to ~ to pay rent	*sich die Miete leisten können*
boring	*langweilig*
clear up doubts	*Zweifel ausräumen*
counter-argument	*Gegenargument*
delicious	*köstlich*
disease	*Krankheit*
dismissal	*Entlassung*
draw lots	*losen*
equity	*Eigenkapital*
esteem	*schätzen*
flu	*Grippe*
lazy	*faul*
middle level	*Mittelbau; mittlere Angestellte*
objection	*Einwand*
obviously	*offensichtlich*
occasion	*Anlass, Gelegenheit*
omnipotence	*Allmacht*
poverty	*Armut*
prayer	*Gebet*
proof	*Beweis*
purpose	*Ziel, Zweck*
refer to	*sich beziehen auf, verweisen auf*
repast	*Mahl*
research	*forschen; untersuchen*
rumour	*Gerücht*
sacrifice	*opfern*
smooth over fears	*Befürchtungen zerstreuen*
spill	*verschütten*
steady job	*feste / sichere Anstellung*
supply	*hier: ausstatten*
supporting evidence	*stützende Beweise*
trainers	*Sportschuhe*
tremble	*zittern*

10 Chapter VISITING THE TRADE FAIR

Tissmann wants to get the feel of a small medical fair in England. He knows that although you don't really sell your products directly, nevertheless customers may place tentative orders for thousands of pounds. Tissy wants to be involved.

Let's start with a smile

At a computer fair, James Kelly was shown a computer that could answer every question. He asked it where his father was. It answered: "Your father is playing poker in a saloon in Las Vegas." "Wrong," said James. "My father is dead and his body lies in a Baptist cemetery in Ohio." The salesman was surprised, and hurriedly typed in: "Where exactly is Mr Kelly senior?" The computer flashed its answer up on the monitor:
"Mr Kelly senior's body lies in a Baptist cemetery in Ohio, but this bastard's father is still sitting in that saloon in Las Vegas."

ATTENTION, PLEASE!

There are five things to improve in the dialogue.
We've marked them in *italics*. Can you correct them?

Checking out MEDIMAKE's booth

MEDIMAKE, like every company, has to present its wares at the major trade fairs. Tissmann wants to participate in the event which is taking place in Manchester. He is particularly interested in MEDIMAKE's electronic range. At the booth in Hall I, Tissmann (T) and John Streven (S), a technical salesman at MEDIMAKE:

T: It's very dynamic here. A lot of things are going on. It's very full. What are the opening hours?
S: 8.30 till 6 p.m. It's a long day.
T: How many visitors do you expect?
S: You mean at the fair? I guess about a quarter of a million.
T: *What you don't say*! Well, how much exhibition space have you rented?
S: Two hundred square metres, but don't ask me what the stand costs. I've got no idea.
T: *I can imagine myself.* I'm very interested in the electronic stuff. Especially the Pulsometer. Have you got a *prospect* for the range?
S: Yes, we have, but I must admit that something went wrong with the documentation this year. We were in too much of a hurry. Several of the photos were out of focus. Several prices were wrongly quoted.
T: Very embarrassing! And couldn't you do *something* about it?
S: Well, it was all too late. The deadline for printing was much too short.
T: Oh well. By the way, I'm interested in your *last* product, this pulsometer. Can you explain it to me, without the documentation?
S: I'll try my best. The Pulsometer is a real innovation. It checks your pulse and your blood pressure. It'll do it when you're standing still, jogging or swimming. If you enter some parameters, height and weight, it tells you how much overweight you are as a percentage. And it'll tell you what sort of sport to do and for how long.
T: Hard to believe!
S: The best part is that the whole equipment is the size of a wristwatch. That's what's really new.
T: Well, you've convinced me. I'll take one.
S: Sorry, Dr Tissmann, but this is a sample. It's not for sale. It's only on display.

TASK 1: Key words in business

Wie sind die Öffnungszeiten?	What are the _________ _____?
Wie viel Ausstellungsfläche haben Sie angemietet?	How much _________ _____ have you _________ ?
Der Termin war zu knapp.	The _________ was too _______ .
Es ist nur ein Ausstellungsstück.	It's only __ _________.
Es hat die Größe einer Armbanduhr.	It is the ______ ___ a wristwatch.
seine Waren vorführen	present one's _________
Die Preisangaben sind falsch.	Prices are _________ _________ .
Die Fotos sind unscharf.	The photos are ___ ___ ________ .
einige Werte eingeben	_________ some _________
ein unverkäufliches Muster	a ________ that is not for ________

TASK 2: Pitfalls for Germans

Could you correct these mistakes?
(See also Task 4 and 5)

1. *What you don't say*!
2. I can *imagine myself*.
3. And you couldn't do *something* about it?
4. I'm interested in your *last* product.
5. Have you got a *prospect* for the range?

TASK 3: Beef up your word power

Where do they fit best?

ware	**product**	**produce**	**goods**

1. Macrosoft presents its _____________at the major trade fairs.
2. It says on the bottle '_____________ of France'.
3. We are marketing a range of beauty _____________ .
4. Should I collect the _____________ , or do you deliver them?
5. The poor devil peddles his handmade ___________ in a street market.

Do you know what these *wares* are? The first has been done for you.

articles made of silver or a metal that look like silver knives, forks, dishes, etc used at meals:	*silverware*
dishes that can be used for cooking food in an oven:	
household equipment and tools, pans, nails, locks and brushes:	
pots, dishes, etc made of baked clay:	

TASK 4: Joke your way round trouble spots

Let's do it with a smile:

(irgend)etwas oder nichts – *something* or *anything*

1. An intellectual is a man who has found ____________ more interesting than women.
2. Never invest your money in ____________ that eats or needs repairing.
   BILLY ROSE
3. Specialists are people who know everything about nothing and nothing about ____________ else.
4. A holiday is ____________ you have for two weeks that takes fifty weeks to pay for.
5. "What's all this fuss about plutonium?" said Annette. "How can ____________ named after a Disney character be dangerous?"
6. An expert is a man who is like a eunuch in a harem – he knows all about it but can't do ____________ about it.
7. The longer one saves ____________ before throwing it away, the sooner it will be needed after it is thrown away.
8. When someone complained to Calvin Coolidge about his habitual silence he replied, "Well, I found out early in life that you didn't have to explain ____________ you didn't say."

TASK 5: More trouble spots to joke around

1. "How much is a chin massage?"
   "£20."
   "But your (*Prospekt*) says £10."
   "Well," the beautician explains, "that is per chin."
2. The (*neuste*) kind of computer was presented at the Cebit in Hannover. Somebody asked it, "What will Germany be like in 2020?" The answer came back in Chinese.
3. Can you (*dir vorstellen*) an entire city under glass? We'd never have to worry about cold or rain or snow again. Just little kids with rocks!
4. A caller who dials the wrong number will call a second time as soon as you have returned to your living room and (*dir gemütlich gemacht hast*).

PHRASES

Master your phrases: At the trade fair

1. Get the right information

Wann wird die Öffentlichkeit zur Messe zugelassen?	When is the fair open to the public?
Wie lange dauert die Ausstellung?	How long will the fair last?
Die Messe ist von 9.30 bis 18.45 geöffnet.	The opening hours of the fair are from 9.30 a.m. to 6.45 p.m.
Haben Sie schon Reservierungen von Firmen aus unserer Branche bekommen?	Have you already received any bookings from firms active in our field?
Kann man im Ausstellerverzeichnis werben?	Is it possible to have advertising in the catalogue?

The art of advertising

If the product sells, it's due to good advertising. If it doesn't, it's due to bad product design.

2. Renting exhibition space

Wir möchten an der Ausstellung teilnehmen.	We'd like to take part in the exhibition.
Wir möchten uns um eine Ausstellungsfläche bewerben.	We wish to apply for exhibition space.
Wie buche ich einen Stand?	How do I book a booth?
Wann ist Anmeldeschluss?	When's the application deadline?
Wie hoch ist die Standmiete?	What's the stand rental?
Können Sie uns ein Angebot für den Quadratmeterpreis machen?	Can you quote us the price per square meter?
Ich möchte einen Stand in der Nähe des Haupteingangs.	I'd like a stand near the main entrance.

3. Trade fair literature

Bitte nehmen Sie uns in den Ausstellerkatalog auf.	Please list us in the exhibitors' catalogue.
Bis wann brauchen Sie das Werbematerial für die Pressemitteilungen?	When do you need the promotional material / sales literature for the press release?
Wann ist letzter Termin für Einträge in den Messekatalog?	When's the deadline for entries in the exhibition catalogue?
Schicken Sie uns bitte den Veranstaltungskalender.	Please send us the calendar of events.
Wie viele Freikarten können Sie uns überlassen?	How many complimentary tickets can you let us have?
Wie viele Ausstellerausweise kann unsere Firma bekommen?	How many badges can our company have?
Die Messeleitung wird die Messeausweise am Montag ausstellen.	The fair authorities will issue the fair passes on Monday.

Advert at a fashion fair

Our clothes not only make girls slim, they also make men look round.

4. Conversation at the booth

Sind dies Werbegeschenke?	Are these freebies / give-aways?
Tut mir Leid, dies ist ein unverkäufliches Muster.	Sorry, but this is a sample. It's not for sale.
Welches Modell verwenden Sie denn zurzeit?	Which model are you using at the moment?
Ich glaube, wir haben genau das Richtige für Sie.	I think we've exactly the right solution for you.
Könnte man das Modell auch für ... verwenden?	Could this model also be used for ...?
Ich führe es Ihnen vor.	Let me demonstrate it to you.
Könnten Sie uns ausführliches Material zu dieser Maschine zusenden?	Could you please send us full details of this machine?
Wir haben mehrere Produkte, die Ihren Anforderungen entsprechen würden.	We've got several products that would meet your requirements.
Haben Sie ein paar Prospekte für mich?	Do you have any brochures I could have?
Sie erhalten auf alle Produkte einen Messerabatt von 15 %.	You get all our products at a trade fair discount of 15 %.
Diese Einführungspreise gelten nur während der Messe.	These introductory prices are only valid during the fair.

Time for a smile

The airline pilot was having his regular medical check.
"When did you last have sex?" asked the doctor as a routine question.
"Nineteen fifty-eight," said the pilot.
"Hell, that was along time ago."
The pilot looked at his watch. "Why? It's only twenty-one fifteen now," he said.

TASK 6: Let's go woggling again

Replace the *woggles* with a suitable word.

1. We'd like to take *woggle* in the exhibition.
2. How long does the fair *woggle*?
3. We wish to apply for *woggle* space.
4. Can you *woggle* us the price per square metre?

TASK 7: Beef up your word power again

Find an expression that has almost the same meaning.

stand	b____
booking	r___________
take part in a fair	p____________ in a fair
free tickets	c______________ tickets

TASK 8: Printed matter

Can you match them?

1 catalogue of	A material
2 sales	B literature
3 promotional	C visitors
4 list of	D exhibitors

Advert seen at the Frankfurt Car Saloon

Perhaps the reason why so many people are satisfied with our cars is because we aren't. HONDA

FOCUS: Getting ready for the fair *

When the products are *researched*, developed and manufacturing is finished it's time to get them to the customer, the more the better. Selling and *distributing* is the next stage of the process. There are several ways of doing this. Sales staff can identify potential customers and get to them. This activity is called *prospecting or canvassing*. Sales departments can place well-timed advertising in journals, newspapers or other media. You can use *direct mailing* where advertising is sent to *prospects* at their *sites.*

erforschen
verteilen
Kundensuche
Direktwerbung
potentielle Kunden; Firmensitz;

Another *distribution* channel is the medium of the trade fair. This is a chance for the sales staff to have a working holiday and drink coffee hour after hour. In this case there are some processes to follow. First, you have to *apply* to exhibition organisers to arrange the conditions of the *rental contract.* You will have to stipulate how much exhibition space you need, check on costs, have your company *included* in the catalogue of *exhibitors* and a lot of other things. Don't forget to apply for *complimentary tickets, badges* and passes allowing you into the building.
Having said this, probably the most valuable part of the trade fair is the opportunity to *talk shop*, or indeed, to make small talk with people and prospects around your *booth.* This is where the networking goes on, which might later put the pennies in your pocket.

Vertrieb
sich wenden an
Mietvertrag
hier: aufnehmen
Aussteller
Freikarte; Anstecker
fachsimpeln
Messestand

WORD AID

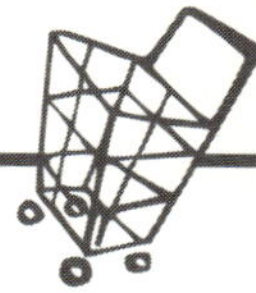

baked clay	*gebrannter Ton*
blood pressure	*Blutdruck*
booth	*(Messe-)Stand*
cemetery	*Friedhof*
chin	*Kinn*
deadline	*letzter Termin*
exhibition space	*Ausstellungsfläche*
fair	*Messe*
guess	*annehmen, raten*
habitual	*gewohnheitsmäßig*
height	*Körpergröße*
involved; be ~	*dabei sein, teilnehmen*
lock	*(Tür-)Schloss*
on display	*zur Ansicht*
participate in	*teilnehmen an*
prospect	*potentieller Kunde*
rock	*Fels, Stein*
sample	*Muster*
satisfied	*zufrieden*
size	*Größe*
slim	*schlank*
tentative order	*vorläufige Bestellung*
wares	*Waren*
weight	*Gewicht*
wristwatch	*Armbanduhr*

11 Chapter

SELLING SUCCESSFULLY

Tissmann feels he should learn more about the English way of selling things, so he has the idea of being involved in a sales discussion at a potential customer's. Watch this space to see how 'Tissy' performs as a salesman! He should read a good book on selling.

A good bargain

The following conversation took place at a Rolls Royce car showroom: "If I buy one of these cars on credit," asked a customer, "how long will I have to pay for it?" – "It depends on how much you can pay each month," replied the salesman. The man paused, "25 pounds, more or less." – "Well then," said the salesman laughing, "it will take you about a hundred years." – "Excellent. Let's sign the contract."

ATTENTION, PLEASE!

There are five things to improve in the dialogue.
We've marked them in *italics*. Can you correct them?

Too many cooks spoil the broth

MEDIMAKE sales in England are generally good. Especially in the areas of certain types of hardware there seems to be a dynamic market. Tissmann (T) wanted to do a benchmarking. He wanted to take similar products, one produced in Germany, one in GB and compare how they are sold. In this case he intended to observe the sales discussion with a potential customer in the English market. He accompanies a star salesman, Nathan Dealer (D), to a rehabilitation centre. Mr Appel (A), chief buyer of the centre, receives them in his office.

D: I'm very grateful you found time to see us today. We won't take longer than absolutely necessary. To cut a long story short, you asked us to tender for ten wheelchairs in varying versions. I believe you've received the documentation and quotations. You've had a week to look through it. Were there any problems?

A: I did look through it, and I must say it's very well-thought through.

T: Well, thank you. It's our company philosophy to present our brochures to serious *undertakers* like yourself as clearly as possible.

D: Yes, well, ehm, that's right. Eh, Mr Appel, you said you might have some special requirements. Perhaps you could ...

A: Yes, of course. I'll tell you straight up that we're interested in six of your Rollsound chairs. We've checked specifications. They fit the bill. We'll have to discuss the quotation of course. These six will be the first of many. But, at the moment another special range is of interest for us. I believe you can help.

T: Yes, our company is much *greater* now and we have several new types of chairs. Nathan will explain.

D: That's right. I ...

A: (interrupting) If I could just ... We're after a sports range. You mention it here in the brochure, but you don't go into detail.

D: Our sports range? Yes, indeed! Let me give you a general idea of the system. Here we're talking about a customised product, the Bronco. I'm sure you'd like to hear about some typical features. Well, this model features many innovations. First of all, 70 per cent of the chair is constructed of aluminium. Light and stable. The wear and tear is negligible. Have a look at the wheels here in the brochure. Specially designed super thin rims.

T: Yes, and all these parts are immediately available in a Global Spare Parts Centre or any good *sports warehouse*.

D: I'm sure Mr Appel knows he can get spare parts from MEDIMAKE at any time. I'm equally sure that you need to know about transporting the wheelchair. Well, the whole thing can be packed together. Look, if you've got time ...

T: And I'd just like to add something here myself. You may have heard that our earlier ranges had some *earnest* problems with toppling over when going round tight corners. Well, that *belongs to the past*. Since then the Bronco has passed the famous turtle test so you can be absolutely certain that nobody will be lying on his back with ...

D: (interrupting). That's well and good, but I guess Mr Appel is more interested in ... (fade out)

TASK 1: Key words in business

einen Vergleichstest machen	do a ________________ (test)
sich um einen Auftrag über zehn Rollstühle bewerben	__________ for ten wheelchairs
Preisangebote erhalten	receive ________________
Wir stellen besondere Anforderungen.	We have special ______________.
Wir haben die technischen Angaben überprüft.	We've ___________ specifications.
Das ist genau das, was wir brauchen.	That _____________the bill.
ein maßgeschneidertes Produkt	a ________________ product
typische Produkteigenschaften	typical ________________
viele Neuerungen aufweisen	______________ many innovations
Den Verschleiß kann man vernachlässigen.	The ______________ is negligible.
Diese Teile sind im zentralen Ersatzteillager erhältlich.	These parts are ______________ in the Spare Parts Centre.

TASK 2: Pitfalls for Germans

Could you correct these mistakes? (See also Task 5 and 6)

1. It's our company philosophy to present our brochures to serious *under-takers* like yourself as clearly as possible.
2. Our company is much *greater* now.
3. Our earlier ranges had some *earnest* problems.
4. These parts are immediately available at any *sports warehouse.*
5. Well, that *belongs to the past.*

TASK 3: Test your memory

1. Why did Tissmann accompany Nathan Dealer?
2. Do you remember the features of the Bronco?
   The chair has specially ____________ super thin rims, it is ______________ of aluminium, is __________ and has recently ____________ the turtle test.

TASK 4: Beef up your word power

Angebot	nach Katalog oder Liste	quotation
	je nach Projekt und Konkurrenz	tender
	allgemein und unspezifisch	offer
	als Verhandlungsbasis, in Anzeigen	ono

1. Four companies have made a tender for the construction work. We will accept the lowest ______________
2. I'm waiting for the latest ____________ from the Stock Exchange.
3. I've had an ____________ of £2,200 for the old Rolls Royce. This is an ____________ that I can't refuse.
4. Advert in the press: Lady's bike £35 ____________.

The difficulty of door-to-door selling

"Dad, there's a man at the door with a moustache." –
"Tell him I've got one."

TASK 5: Joke your way round trouble spots

One word in German – two words in English. Which fits best?

ernst(haft)	earnest(ly)
	serious(ly)

1. The ______________ music lover is the bloke who, hearing a soprano in the bathroom, puts his ear to the keyhole.
2. A famous English entrepreneur once said to an applicant for the job of accountant: "In your testimonials it says you're are an extremely ______________ fellow, without imagination and a 'yes-man' with no sense of humour at all. In most professions all these things would be a ______________ drawback. In accountancy they are a positive asset."
3. I have come to the conclusion that politics is too ______________ a matter to be left to the politicians.
   CHARLES DE GAULLE
4. The best way to tell if a man is honest is to ______________ ask him if he is honest. If he says he is, you know he's a crook.

TASK 6: More trouble spots to joke through

One word in German – four words in English. Which fits best?

groß	big	tall
	large	great

1. Napoleon may not have been a ______________ man, but for many he was a ______________ statesman.
2. My aunt hid a ______________ sum of money and jewellery before she died. My lawyer has arranged a seance with a medium to inquire about its whereabouts.
3. Adolescence: the period in which the young suddenly feel a ______________ responsibility to answer the telephone.
4. If you are a ______________ enough company, your mistakes become standards. Just take the example of Microsoft.

Master your phrases: Sales talk

1. Exchanging polite noises

Ich weiß, dass Sie eine sehr beschäftigte Frau sind.	I appreciate that you're a very busy woman.
Ich bin dankbar, dass Sie für mich Zeit gefunden haben.	I'm grateful you found time to see me.
Danke, dass Sie uns etwas von Ihrer wertvollen Zeit widmen.	Thank you for sparing us your valuable time.
Ich werde Sie wirklich nicht lange aufhalten. Deshalb werden wir uns kurz fassen.	I really won't take too much of your time. So we will be brief.
Kommen wir gleich zur Sache.	Let's come straight to the point.
Seien Sie versichert, dass wir Ihren Bedarf genau erfüllen können.	I'd like to assure you that we can meet your needs quite exactly.

Food for thought

Never simply say: "Sorry, we don't have what you are looking for."
Always say: "Too bad, I just sold the last one today." ROBERT SKOLE

2. Referring to your brochures

Ich weiß nicht, ob Sie sich daran erinnern, dass Sie von uns einen Katalog erhalten haben.	I don't know whether you remember getting our catalogue.
In der Zwischenzeit dürften Sie unsere Informationen über ... bekommen haben.	Now, in the meantime you should have received our brochures about ...
Unsere Informationsmappe sagt alles über uns.	Our information pack explains all about us.

3. Refer to preparatory talks

Zuerst würde ich gerne auf ein paar Punkte zurückkommen, die Sie mir neulich genannt haben.	First, I'd like to go back over a couple of points you mentioned to me the other day.
Ich habe die Anforderungen durchgesehen, die Sie mir letzte Woche geschildert haben.	I've been checking through the requirements you described to me last week.
Sie erwähnten, dass Sie zehn XL-Kopierer brauchen könnten.	You mentioned that you might need about ten XL copiers.
Unser Kopierer hat alle Vergleichstests bestanden.	Our copier has passed all the benchmarking tests.
Wenn Sie gestatten, fasse ich zusammen, was wir am Telefon vereinbart haben.	If you allow me, sir, I'll just recap what we agreed on the phone.

TASK 7: Complete the dialogue

Customer	**Salesman**
Pleased to meet you.	The ______________ is mine.
I'm afraid I can't spare you more than an hour.	Well, let's ______________ to the point.
What we need are customised wheelchairs.	I assure you that we can ________ your ______________ exactly.
What about your competitors?	Our wheelchair has __________ all the ___________________ .

The USP – the unique selling proposition

A salesman knocked at the door of a house in Wimbledon. "Good morning," he said. "Would you care to buy a copy of 'Five Hundred Excuses To Give Your Wife For Staying Out Late'?" – "Why on earth would I want a book like that?" said the lady. – "Because," replied the salesman, "I sold a copy to your husband at his office this morning."

FOCUS: What selling is all about

Nothing ever happens unless someone sells something to someone else. Products would sit in *warehouses* for eternity. People would become unemployed. We would all be leading isolated little lives, *striving* to make a living. Or would we even own the land, if there were no one to sell it to us? *Skills* can be learned and trained, *qualities* not – you must have them. Before you hire a salesman, find out if he suits the "Hire-Formula".

Warenlager
streben
Fertigkeiten
Eigenschaften

The Hire-Formula

H*onesty*: no hiding of facts; keeping one's promises — *Ehrlichkeit*
I*ndustry*: the quality of working hard — *Fleiß*
Resilience: the quality of recovering quickly from a *setback* — *Rückschlag*
E*mpathy*: the ability to share another person's feelings as if they were your own. — *Einfühlungsvermögen*

And as far as skills go a salesman must be "pepsi". This might be *acquired* in seminars. — *erwerben*

The Pepsi-Formula

People skills: psychological know-how in dealing with customers
E*fficiency*: doing one's task successfully without wasting time, energy and money — *Effektivität*
P*ersuasion*: being able to give the customer reasons to buy from you — *Überredungskunst*
System: working and organising by following a plan or a method
Initiative: making decisions or taking actions without waiting for someone to tell you what to do.

The Icarus-Formula

Here is an *overview* of six main aspects of the selling process. After you have *acquired* a good knowledge of your products, their *strengths* and weaknesses, you should do the same for your competitors' products. Then follow our Icarus-Formula	*Überblick* *gewinnen* *Stärken*
Identify customers: Find the right potential buyer for what you're selling. When you're selling yourself into a new job, it means finding the right potential *employer.*	*Arbeitgeber*
Contact customers: You've been invited to visit a customer. Remember, you never get a second chance to make a good first impression.	
Ask the right questions: Read your client's literature. Ask for permission to *take notes*. Find out about interests, needs, personal and company *goals*, their experiences with your competitors.	*Notizen machen* *Ziele*
Representing your company and your product *requires* the most preparation. Practise your answers to questions with a close friend. Make a list of your strongest qualities.	*erfordern*
Use the information you *obtained* in step three to meet *concerns* your client may have. Counterbalance them with the *benefits* of your product. If you side-step objections you won't establish a lasting relationship. Find out how important *objections* are and suggest a solution.	*erhalten, erlangen; Bedenken* *Kundenvorteil* *Einwand*
Sell: Don't press for a contract! *Closing* the sale should follow smoothly after addressing concerns.	*abschließen*

Structure your sales talk

1. Give a general idea

Let's get a general idea of the product.
Basically, what the system does, is ...
This system is mainly used in / for ...

2. Say what is special about it

One of its outstanding features is ...
The main advantages of our service are ...
The primary characteristic of the product is ...

3. Describe features that are important to the customer

The wear and tear is negligible.
It is robust and reliable.
It is easy to maintain and to handle.

4. Appeal to instincts

Few people want to have the old model of anything.
It's a matter of prestige, status, pride or fear.

This is the latest design.
The technology is highly advanced ...
All the functions are state of the art ...
It replaces all the previous models.

5. Present testimonials

It has been rated best in three consumer reports.
It has been proven in many tests.
This wheelchair has passed the turtle test.
It has passed all the benchmarking tests.

Watch your language

Many words *common to* selling situations can generate fearful or negative associations in the clients' minds. For example, don't use words like 'buy' or 'price'. The same *holds true for* 'sell' and 'sold'. Nobody wants to be sold something. The customer will associate them with money. He'll see his hard-earned cash leaving his pockets and going into your pockets. *Down payment* is even worse and *instalment plan* reminds him that he will have to pay *interest* because hasn't the money to pay the full price now. And don't say 'Would you please put your signature under this *contract*?' Contracts have to do with lawyers, jargon, clauses, *deadlines* and *fine print*. A signature is final and binds him to the terms of contract. All these words are losers. Replace them with winners. Winners create positive mental images. Who wouldn't like to 'make an investment', *own* something, be in a position of *authorising* others or get an agreement? Here are a few suggestions:

üblich in
gelten für
Anzahlung
Ratenzahlungsplan; Zinsen
Vertrag
Termine; Kleingedrucktes
besitzen; autorisieren

Losers	Winners
Wouldn't you like to *buy* this ship?	Wouldn't you like to *own* this ship?
We've *sold* over a thousand of this model.	More than a thousand customers have *acquired* this model.
The *down payment* is £100.	Your *initial investment* is £100.
Let's have a look at the *contract*.	Let's look at the *agreement* (paperwork, form).
Would you please *sign* / put your *signature* under / the *contract*?	Would you please give me an *authorisation for the agreement*?

How to sell effectively

One door-to-door salesman does very well by using the opening line: "Can I interest you in something your neighbour said you couldn't possibly afford?"

WORD AID

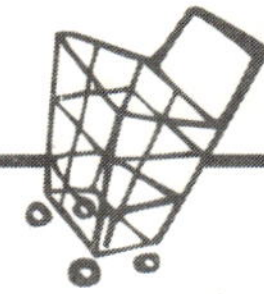

acquire	*erwerben*
afford; be able to ~	*sich leisten können*
asset	*Vorteil; Aktivposten*
available	*verfügbar*
benchmarking test	*Vergleichstest (mit der Konkurrenz)*
bloke	*Bursche*
broth; too many cooks spoil the ~	*zu viele Köche verderben den Brei*
crook	*Schurke*
customised	*maßgeschneidert*
down payment	*Anzahlung*
entrepreneur	*Unternehmer*
honest	*ehrlich*
intend	*beabsichtigen*
maintain	*warten, unterhalten*
mention	*erwähnen*
quotation	*Angebot*
responsibility	*Verantwortung*
rim	*Felge*
seance	*Sitzung*
spare parts	*Ersatzteile*
tender	*ein Preisangebot machen*
testimonials	*Referenzen; Empfehlungen*
topple over	*umkippen*
undertaker	*Leichenbestatter*
warehouse	*Lager*
wear and tear	*Verschleiß*

12 Chapter MASTERING MEETINGS*

In modern companies, managing has to do with communication. One important vehicle for communication is the meeting. Some managers spend as much as 60 per cent of their time at meetings. But, as everybody knows, meetings can turn into a horror show. For example, the agenda is not kept, minutes are not taken accurately, there is argument instead of productive discussion, and a lot more.

How to master the meeting

"There are two sides to every question," said the new boss at the first meeting, "my side and the wrong side. And don't say 'yes' until I've finished."

ATTENTION, PLEASE!

There are some things to improve in the dialogue. We've marked them in *italics*. Can you correct them?

Not an ordinary set of scales

Dr Tissmann, (T) who is now half an Englishman (he has been in England more than three months by now), has joined a meeting on the topic of discounts and commissions when selling a certain product range, the Mediscale. Jim Carpenter (C) is chairing the meeting, also attending are Tom Shaw (S), Head of Sales, and Bert Dune (D) from Finances.

C: (fade in) ... and so if everyone has received a copy of the agenda, perhaps we can begin with our topic number one, the Viagram range. Tom, perhaps you can give us a summary of the matter?

S: Certainly. Well, basically we've run into some serious problems concerning the Viagram range.

T: *What for* problems? Last week I *have visited* the *fabric* and I was particularly impressed how efficiently and in what excellent quality the scales were erected.

D: Thank you, Uwe, but that's not the point. The problem is that customers don't seem to want to buy them.

S: That's it! The range consists of four pieces, the Viagram-Standard, the Viagram-Plus, the Viagram-De-Luxe and the Audio-Viagram-Master. The latter is a computerised scale. Not only does it weigh you to an accuracy of point five of a gram, it also tells you the percentage of your body liquids and your body fat. It makes a prognosis of what you should eat. And the information is also delivered by a loudspeaker so the candidate cannot close his eyes to his fat reality.

C: And what is more, R&D is developing a diagnostic scale, the Viagram-Super, that can tell you age, sex, life expectancy and ...

T: (interrupting) Sex life? How *ordinary*! I'm sure I don't wish *each* Tom, Dick and Harry to know about my sex life and body data.

C: Now, now, Uwe, let's keep to the subject, shall we?

S: And that subject is, in my opinion, that we've got to stimulate our potential customers by offering bigger discounts to our dealers.

T: But the Viagram range is already cheap enough. And don't forget the generous *provision* that the dealers get.

D: From a financial point of view, Uwe is right. We are cheap and our profit margin is minimal. Perhaps we should be looking at other strategies.

T: Right! And my suggestion would be to go back to the customers and *inquire* about what they really need.

S: My God, it's too late for all that (fade out) ...

TASK 1: Key words in business

große Probleme bekommen	___ ______ serious problems
Waagen rationell montieren	__________ scales efficiently
potenzielle Kunden anregen	________ our _______ customers
Händlern Rabatte anbieten	offer __________ to __________
Die Produktreihe besteht aus vier Elementen.	The product range __________ of four pieces.
Die Gewinnspanne ist minimal.	The profit __________ is minimal.

TASK 2: Pitfalls for Germans

Could you correct these mistakes?

1. *What for* problems?
2. Last week I *have visited* the *fabric.*
3. Sex life? How *ordinary*!
4. I don't wish *each* Tom, Dick and Harry to know my body data.
5. And don't forget the generous *provision* that the dealers get.
6. And my suggestion would be to go back to the customers and *inquire* about what they really need.

TASK 3: Test your memory

1. What are the problems discussed at the meeting? Tick them off.
   - ❑ low profit margins
   - ❑ high discounts for dealers
   - ❑ low quality
   - ❑ teething problems
   - ❑ weak demand
   - ❑ no customer orientation
2. Why is Tissmann against the Viagram-Super?

TASK 4: Joke your way round trouble spots

One phrase in German – two phrases in English

Was für ein(e)...	What a ... What ...

1. Jean Dupont sold the Venus de Milo a spray deodorant. (*Was für ein*) salesman!
2. Director to speaker: Your vocabulary is limited in words, but (*was für ein*) turnover!
3. Tailor: "Your suit will be ready in six weeks, sir."
   Client: "Six weeks! But God made the whole world in only six days."
   Tailor: Quite true, sir. But look (*was für ein*) state it is in."
4. A Russian student of economics was sent to the United States to study the death of capitalism. Back home his professor asked him, "What are your conclusions?"
   "(*Was für ein*) wonderful way to die!" sighed the student.
5. Customer: May I have a pair of alligator shoes?
   Salesman: Certainly. (*Was für eine Größe hat*) your alligator?

TASK 5: More trouble spots to joke around

One word in German – two words in English

jede / r / s	each every

1. Boss: "It hasn't escaped me that (*jedes Mal*) Liverpool is playing at home mid-week you ask permission to go and visit your grandmother who's seriously ill."
   John: "What a coincidence. But you don't think, by any chance, she's faking it?"
2. "What are we going to do with this batch of a hundred coats from last year?" asked the shop assistant. "We've marked them down to a pound (*ein jedes*) but they still won't sell."
   "Use your head!" replied the boss. "Price them at two pounds (*jedes*).

Send six out to (*jedem*) of our best clients, but put in an invoice for only five. They'll think we've made a mistake and jump at the bargain."
Two weeks later the shop assistant comes rushing into his boss's office. "Can you imagine! (*Jeder*) customer returned the parcel along with the invoice, but only five coats!"

3. Did you hear about the Irish buyer?
He ordered two chinchillas for his wife. One for (*jedes*) chin.

PHRASES

Master your phrases: Getting through at meetings

1. Opening the meeting

Meine Damen und Herren, ich erkläre die Sitzung für eröffnet.	Ladies and Gentlemen, I declare the meeting open.
Ich habe die Ehre, die erste Sitzung des Komitees für ... eröffnen zu dürfen.	I have the honour of declaring the first session of the committee on ... open.
Im Namen der Unternehmungsleitung darf ich Sie herzlich begrüßen.	On behalf of the management allow me to extend a warm welcome to you.

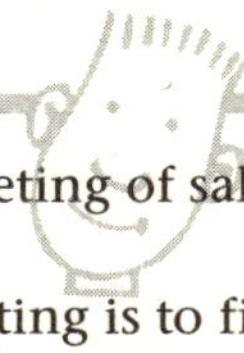

The President of a big company opened up a meeting of salesmen by announcing:
"Ladies and Gentlemen, the purpose of this meeting is to fire you with enthusiasm. If it doesn't work I'm going to fire you – with enthusiasm."

2. The agenda

Haben alle eine Kopie der Tagesordnung erhalten?	Has everyone received a copy of the agenda?
Möchte jemand noch einen Punkt auf die Tagesordnung setzen?	Would anybody wish to add an item / point to the agenda?

Diese Frage wird unter Punkt 5 behandelt.	This question is already covered under item 5.
Könnten wir Punkt 3 der Tagesordnung streichen?	Could we delete item 3 from the agenda?
Der erste Punkt der Tagesordnung ist ...	The first item on the agenda is ...

3. The minutes

Haben alle eine Kopie des Protokolls der letzten Besprechung?	Has everybody got a copy of the minutes of our last meeting?
Können wir das Protokoll als angenommen betrachten?	Can we take the minutes as read?
Wer führt heute das Protokoll?	Who is going to keep the minutes today?

A meeting should consist of three men, two of whom are absent.
ROBERT COPELAND

4. Explaining the purpose

Das Thema unserer Besprechung ist ...	The subject of our meeting is ...
Der Grund unseres Beisammenseins ist ...	The reason for our gathering / coming together is ...
Womit wir uns heute befassen müssen, ist ...	What we need / have to deal with today is ...
Was wir heute diskutieren / erörtern wollen, ist ...	What we want to discuss / consider today is ...
Drei Probleme sollten heute gelöst werden.	There are three problems that should be solved today.
Heute müssen drei Entscheidungen gefällt werden.	There are three decisions to be taken today.

5. Any other business

Sonstiges	Any Other Business (A.O.B.)
Gibt es sonst noch etwas?	Is there any other business?
Noch irgendwelche Punkte?	Any further points?
Gibt es sonst noch etwas zu besprechen?	Is there anything else to discuss?
Noch irgendwelche Punkte, bevor wir die Sitzung schließen?	Any further points before we bring this meeting to an end?

Once the chairman of the Board of Directors visited one of his directors in hospital. "Bob," he said, "the Board of Directors wishes you a speedy recovery – and it was a majority decision of seven to five."

6. Putting it to the vote

Stimmen wir darüber ab.	Let's have a vote on this.
Bringen wir es zur Abstimmung.	Let's put it to the vote.
Darf ich um Handzeichen bitten?	Can I ask for a show of hands?
Wer dafür ist, möge die Hand heben.	Those in favour raise their hands.
Wer dafür ist, stimme mit 'ja'.	Those in favour say 'Aye'.
Wer ist dagegen?	Those against?
Wer enthält sich der Stimme?	Any abstentions?
Der Antrag ist mit sieben zu vier Stimmen angenommen.	The motion is carried by seven votes to four.
Der Antrag ist mit acht zu drei Stimmen abgelehnt.	The motion is rejected by eight votes to three.

7. The meeting is closed

Gut, ich glaube, wir haben alles berücksichtigt.	Well, I think we've covered everything.
Nun, damit haben wir die Tagesordnung abgeschlossen.	Well, I think that completes our agenda.
Wenn niemand mehr etwas zu sagen hat, würde ich die Besprechung gerne schließen.	If nobody has anything to add, I'd like to draw the meeting to an end.
Ich möchte allen für ihre konstruktiven Beiträge danken.	I'd like to thank everyone for their constructive contributions.
Ich erkläre die Sitzung für geschlossen.	I declare the meeting closed.
Das ist alles für heute. Vielen Dank.	That's all for today. Thank you.

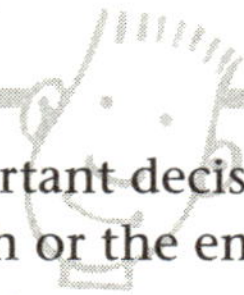

Regardless of the length of the meeting, all important decisions will be made in the last five minutes before lunch or the end of the day.

TASK 6: Let's woggle around meetings

Replace the *woggles* with a suitable word.

1. Ladies and Gentlemen, I *woggle* the meeting open.
2. Would anybody wish to *woggle* an item / point to the agenda?
3. Who is going to *woggle* the minutes today?
4. There are three decisions to be *woggled* today.
5. Is there any other *woggle*?
6. Let's *woggle* it to the vote.
7. The motion is *woggled* by seven votes to four.

The great economist Adam Smith's last words were:
"I believe we must adjourn the meeting to some other place."

▶ FOCUS: Meetings in Britain*

In Britain the meeting is the most important and *time-consuming* management *tool.* It is considered as a part of the work and not as a *necessary evil.* Even unimportant decisions are discussed, voted and *put into practice.* An important meeting is *scheduled* well in advance and a detailed agenda is *distributed* to all participants. Not everybody will have read it or come to the meeting well-prepared. However, everybody is expected to make a *contribution,* if only by asking questions, giving their opinion and listening patiently to the *views* of colleagues.

Only the most formal meetings are opened and closed on time. The majority of meetings are *informal* in style and begin and end with small talk. However, it is not acceptable to leave in the middle of a meeting, make or take phone calls or get on with paperwork.

Discussions may be *controversial.* But it is the chairperson's *concern* to avoid *irreconcilable* clashes. Loyalty to the boss and the company is stronger than even fundamental disagreement.

A meeting without some concrete result is regarded as a *failure.* However, it is considered fair play not to influence members beforehand in order to *bring about* a decision with the help of a lobby. It is usual first to listen to the arguments of the others and then *support* a suggestion.

Of course, there may be some *exceptions* to the rule, especially in politics. After all, it was a Brit who invented the lobby.

zeitraubend
Instrument
notwendiges Übel
verwirklichen
ansetzen
verteilen
Beitrag
Ansichten
zwanglos
kontrovers
Sorge; unversöhnlich
Misserfolg
herbeiführen
unterstützen
Ausnahme

* More about British business culture in John Mole, *Mind Your Manners,* Nicholas Brealy Publishing: London 1995.

WORD AID

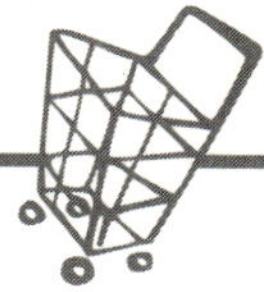

adjourn	*vertagen*
agenda	*Tagesordnung*
batch	*Posten, Charge*
coincidence	*Zufall; Zusammentreffen*
customer	*Kunde*
dealer	*Händler*
deliver	*liefern*
erect	*montieren, zusammenbauen*
expectancy; life ~	*Lebenserwartung*
fabric	*Gewebe, Stoff*
fat	*Fett*
inquire (enquire)	*untersuchen*
invoice	*Rechnung*
jump at a bargain	*sich auf ein Schnäppchen stürzen*
liquid	*Flüssigkeit; flüssig*
mark a product down	*ein Produkt herabsetzen*
minutes (of a meeting)	*Protokoll*
permission	*Erlaubnis*
profit margin	*Gewinnspanne*
purpose	*Zweck, Ziel*
recovery	*Genesung*
regardless of	*ungeachtet*
speedy	*schnell*
suggestion	*Vorschlag*
summary	*Zusammenfassung*
tailor	*Schneider*
turnover	*Umsatz*
vehicle	*Mittel; Fahrzeug*
weigh	*wiegen*

13 Chapter SUCCESSFUL PRESENTATION*

Making presentations is something the thought of which puts the fear of God into some speakers. They can't sleep for several nights before the presentation. We have to find ways of overcoming our nervousness, of creating a good atmosphere, of keeping the interested attention of our listeners. The bad news is that it is not always easy to be in full command of our own behaviour and body language while presenting. The good news is, nobody is perfect. We can learn by observing others. We all do something or other wrong while presenting. No need to worry! Good luck!

Time for a smile

To help a new salesman become familiar with the company's product, the sales manager suggested he demonstrate it to his wife. The next morning the manager asked, "How did the presentation go?"

"I did what you told me," said the salesman, "and when I finished, I asked my wife, 'Would you buy it?' She said, 'Yes'! When I asked her why, she replied, 'Because I love you'!"

ATTENTION, PLEASE!

There are some things to improve in the text.
We've marked them in *italics*. Can you correct them?

* Lernen Sie die Kunst des Präsentierens mit *Get Through at Meetings. Business English für Konferenzen und Präsentationen*, rororo sprachen, auch mit Audio-CD.

The Body & Soul Styler

Dr Tissmann was asked to make a presentation of a new piece of equipment just launched on the market by MEDIQUIP in Highdelmountain. His English colleagues were very eager to hear his description of the latest MEDIQUIP product, the Body & Soul Styler. Tissmann, in the conference room of the Victoria Hotel, Nottingham.

Well, Ladies and Gentlemen,

Before I describe the topic of this presentation I'd like to apologise for the quality of my English. Even though I've been here almost four months it's more difficult than I thought to say exactly what I mean. Forgive me if I *do* any mistakes. To err is human, as the saying goes.
Okay! Today the topic of this presentation is the Body & Soul Styler. As you know it's brand new on the market.
First of all I *try* to give you an overview of this very innovative product. Then we can have question time because, I'm sure there are lots of things you'll want to know. Right! To start with, I'll give a brief description of this range, then I'll *declare* its features and advantages, and finally we can discuss where we see the future and the markets for this equipment.
Well, I'll begin by showing you a photograph of the Body & Soul Styler. In the centre of the picture you can see a gentleman. He looks relaxed and very well trained. The reason for his superman-like appearance is our company's *politic* to design and manufacture instruments which optimise all our organs and muscles. And with the Body & Soul Styler that is exactly what we have done.
Here on the next transparency in the top left you can see the device around the neck of the athlete. *How does it look*? Just like a necklace. No problem at all. Our clients will see it as an ornament, a decoration for the body. Well, it's a small watch on a leather string. And of course, this small watch has very special functions. It'll show your blood pressure, pulse rate, body temperature.
"But what are the real benefits, the innovative features?" you're certainly asking yourselves. Well, can you imagine that when you're walking around with the Body & Soul Styler, it warns you when you're getting under stress. It then advises you what to do to get down to an optimal

level of stress. This can include a few useful *advices* such as "go to the swimming pool in the next ten minutes", "throw that steak down the nearest toilet", and "tell that young woman to put her clothes back on immediately". The Body & Soul Styler is very *human* and also has proposals as to how the stressed manager can make connections to partners who are ... (fade out)

TASK 1: Key words in business

ein Gerät	a piece of ____________
auf den Markt bringen	____________ on the market
nagelneu auf dem Markt	_________________ on the market
Kontakte zu Partnern herstellen	____________ connections to partners
Welches sind die Vorzüge?	____________ the ____________ ?

TASK 2: Phrases for presenters

eine Präsentation machen	____________ a presentation
Das Thema dieser Präsentation ist...	The ____________ of this presentation is ...
einen Überblick über das Produkt geben	give an ____________ of the product
ein Foto zeigen	____________ a photograph
Zeit für Fragen haben	____________ question ____________

Advice from the expert

It's hard to feel as fit as a fiddle
when you're shaped like a cello.

Nothing is better for the spirit or body than a love affair.
It elevates the thoughts and flattens stomachs.

TASK 3: Pitfalls for Germans

(See also Task 5 and 6)

Tricky words and phrases

1. Then I'll *declare* its features and advantages.
2. *How does it look?*
3. The Body & Soul Styler is very *human* and also has proposals as to how the stressed manager can make connections to partners.
4. The reason for his superman-like appearance is our company's *politics* to design and manufacture instruments which optimise all our organs and muscles.
5. Forgive me if I *do* any mistakes.

Tricky Grammar

6. First of all *I try* to give you an overview of this very innovative product.
7. This can include a few useful *advices* such as "go to the swimming pool in the next ten minutes".

TASK 4: Test your memory

Are these statements true or false? The first has been done for you.

	True	False
1. The new product is best suited for fitness centres.		✔
2. The device is worn round the chest.		
3. It prevents you from getting overweight.		
4. It has social functions, too.		

How to win the attention of the audience

I am here to speak to you, you are here to listen to me.
If you finish first, please let me know.

TASK 5: Joke your way round trouble spots

One word in German – three words in English

wie	as
	how
	what

1. A true gentleman is someone who knows (*wie*) to play the trumpet but doesn't.
2. The director had never been so upset as when Margaret asked (*wie*) he wanted to name the baby. Margaret, that's his secretary.
3. Money isn't everything. There are other things, such (*wie*) jewellery, stocks and travellers cheques.
4. Funny (*wie*) a wife can spot a blonde hair on a chap's coat, yet miss the garage doors.
5. When Noah sailed the waters blue,
   he had his troubles same (*wie*) you.
   For forty days he drove the Ark
   before he found a place to park.

How to break the ice

Before I begin my speech I'd like to warn you that I'm suffering from a severe handicap –
I'm sober.

TASK 6: More trouble spots to joke around

One word in German – four words in English.

Fehler	error
	defect
	flaw
	mistake

Your turn! If there's more than one solution, choose the one that fits best.

1. Fred was stunned by the news of his wife's pregnancy. "It's impossible," he lamented. "I'm always so careful. How could it possibly happen?" – "There, there," she consoled him "who says it was your _______________ ?"
2. All great discoveries are made by _______________.
3. Nature always sides with the hidden _______________. Unfortunately, the hidden _______________never remains hidden.
4. The only real _______________ are human _______________.
5. A doctor can bury his _______________. An architect can only advise his client to plant vines.
6. A _______________ will not occur till a machine has passed final inspection.
7. Any _______________ in any calculation will be in the direction of most harm.
8. No one is listening until you make a _______________.

Master your phrases: Handling presentations

1. Announcing the subject

Wie Sie wissen, bin ich hier, um Ihnen ... vorzustellen.	As you know, I'm here to present ... to you.
In meiner Präsentation werde ich unser neues Projekt erläutern.	In my presentation I'll be explaining our new project.
Heute früh will ich einen Rückblick auf das letzte Geschäftsjahr geben.	This morning I'd like to look back at the past fiscal year.

How to thank the presenter for the handouts

Many thanks for your documentation.
I'll lose no time in reading it.

2. Referring to handouts

Darf ich Ihre Aufmerksamkeit auf die Tischvorlage vor Ihnen lenken?	May I draw your attention to the handout in front of you?
In den Tischvorlagen, die ich herumgehen lasse, finden Sie ...	In the handout which I'll be passing round you'll find ...
Wie Sie alle Ihren Unterlagen entnommen haben, die Sie vorab erhalten haben ...	As you all know from your pre-conference handouts ...

3. Giving an overview

Meine Präsentation gliedert sich in drei Teile.	My presentation will be in three main parts.
Ich werde Ihnen die wichtigsten Stufen unseres Projekts schildern.	I'll be developing the major stages of our project.
Zuerst würde ich gerne ... Zweitens könnten wir ... Und ich werde schließen mit ...	Firstly, I'd like to ... Secondly, we could ... And I'll finish with ...

4. Structure your presentation

Ich möchte zuerst etwas über ... sagen.	I'd like to start by saying something about ...
Ich möchte Ihnen zuerst eine allgemeine Vorstellung von ... geben.	First, I'd like to give you a general idea / picture of ...
Ich beginne mit einer Zusammenfassung der Probleme, die wir mit ... haben.	I'll begin by summarising the problems we're having with ...

5. Announcing the next step

Als Nächstes will ich mich auf ... konzentrieren.	Next I'd like to concentrate on ...
Der nächste Punkt, den ich behandeln möchte ist ...	The next point I wish to deal with is ...
Ich komme nun zu meinem nächsten Thema / Punkt / Frage.	I'd like to move on to my next subject / point / item / issue.

6. Using visual material

Bevor ich beginne, können alle die Leinwand sehen?	Well, before I start, can everybody see the screen?
Wie Sie dem ersten Bild / Diagramm entnehmen können ...	As you can see in picture one / in diagram one ...
Das nächste Dia zeigt ...	The next slide shows ...
Diese Kurve zeigt / stellt ... dar.	This curve represents ...
Wenn wir diese beiden Kurven vergleichen, dann ...	If we compare these two curves, then ...

7. Announcing the end

Damit komme ich mit meinem Beitrag zum Schluss.	Well, that completes my part.
Lassen Sie mich mit den Worten schließen ...	Let me end by saying that ...
Ich möchte mit der Feststellung schließen, dass ...	I'd like to conclude by saying that ...

Time for a smile

At the end of a presentation, the chairman rose and said, "Your presentation has not left me any the wiser." The presenter retorted, "Perhaps not wiser, sir, but better informed."

8. Summarising

In einem Wort ...	To put it in a nutshell ...
Wenn ich zusammenfassen darf ...	If I may summarise ...
Schauen wir uns noch einmal die wichtigsten Punkte an.	Let us go over the main points again.
Zusammenfassend können wir also sagen, dass	So to summarise we can say that ...

9. Saying good-bye

So, das war's für heute. Vielen Dank für Ihre Aufmerksamkeit.	So that's all for today. Thank you for your attention.
Es war mir ein Vergnügen, zu Ihnen zu sprechen.	It's been a pleasure talking to you.
Danke, dass Sie gekommen sind.	Thank you for being here.

What you should not say to the presenter

Your presentation has been most entertaining. Are there any hard facts to follow?

TASK 7: Visual aids for presentations

What are they in English?

Dia	Folie
Tischvorlage	Diagramm
Leinwand	Grafik

TASK 8: Word builder's corner

Say it with a verb.

What's the *explanation* for this?	How can we .... this?
What are the *benefits* from this situation?	How can we .... from this situation?
What are the *implications*?	What does this .... ?

TASK 9: Tense and aspect

Can you get the verb forms right?

1. Mr X (*speak*) to you about marketing on the Internet.
2. I (*be*) a consultant to IBM for three years.
3. I (*try*) to give you an overview of our activities.
4. In the handout I (*pass*) round, you (*find*) all the figures.

How to evaluate the presenter

Excellent:	He talks like a god.
Good:	He talks like an angel.
Average:	He talks to himself.
Unsatisfactory:	He argues with himself.
Hopeless:	He loses the argument.

▶ FOCUS: The language of presentations

Most people prepare their presentation in writing. The result is more often than not a written paper and not a presentation. Don't forget that your audience is doing you a favour by listening to you. They want to be talked to, so don't read them a paper. Here are some rules you should observe.

- When preparing your presentation, don't copy from catalogues or specifications. They are written English.
- Learning your presentation by heart is almost as bad as reading it to the audience.
- Use your own words and have them checked by one of the native speakers in your company or an English trainer.

Here are a few examples:

Avoid written style	Use spoken English
A, B, C The Intelligent Robot is two metres tall, weighs 200 KGs, has a new generation of brains, the gift of speech.	A and B and C Our Intelligent Robot is two metres tall *and* weighs 200 KGs, *and* he has a new generation of brains *and* most important of all he has the gift of speech.
Third person: He, they *Participants* at meetings will have experienced of how tiring it is to listen to a presentation that is read by the presenter.	First or second person: I, you *You* are in a meeting and the presenters doesn't talk to you. He reads his paper. And what happens? *You* doze off after a few minutes. *I* think you all know what *I* mean.
Avoid abstract phrases *The user* of the traditional domestic equipment will have encountered disagreeable *failures*.	Call a spade a spade *I* suppose *you* know that sort of unpleasant surprise. You bought a *cheap vacuum cleaner* and when you tried it at home it started *blowing instead of sucking*.

WORD AID

advise	*beraten*
appearance	*Aussehen, Erscheinung*
audience	*Publikum*
become familiar with	*vertraut werden mit*
benefit	*Vorteil, Gewinn*
body language	*Körpersprache*
brand new	*nagelneu*
brief	*kurz*
call a spade a spade	*die Dinge beim Namen nennen*
console	*trösten*
declare	*behaupten*
decoration	*Schmuck*
doze off	*einnicken*
elevate someone's thoughts	*jemanden inspirieren*
err	*irren*
fiddle; as fit as a ~	*gesund wie ein Fisch im Wasser*
flatten	*flach machen*
gift of speech	*Redegabe*
harm	*Schaden*
heart; learn by ~	*auswendig lernen*
jewellery	*Schmuck*
lament	*klagen*
launch on the market	*auf den Markt bringen*
make connections	*Kontakte anknüpfen*
observe	*beobachten*
observe rules	*Regeln beachten*
ornament	*Zierde, Schmuck*
overweight	*Übergewicht, übergewichtig*
participants	*Teilnehmer*
plant / grow wine	*Wein anbauen*
prevent someone from doing ...	*jemanden daran hindern, etwas zu tun ...*
proposal	*Vorschlag*

pulse rate	*Pulsfrequenz*
remain hidden	*verborgen bleiben*
retort	*erwidern*
sober	*nüchtern*
spot	*ausmachen, erspähen*
stomach	*Bauch, Magen*
stunned	*verdutzt*
suffer from	*leiden an*
suggest	*vorschlagen*
suited; best ~ for	*am besten geeignet für*
topic	*Thema*
transparency	*Folie*
trumpet	*Trompete*
upset; be ~	*verstört sein*

CROSS-CULTURAL DIFFICULTIES

Chapter 14

It's sometimes difficult enough to really communicate with people within one's own country. There are different ways of behaving, different accents, different social backgrounds etc. It's all the more difficult when business has to cross borders. Not only the language problem comes to torture us, but also different habits, morals and attitudes. One man's meat is another man's poison.

Time for a smile

At a computer congress a Japanese gentleman was sitting in the cafeteria next to a delegate from Texas. After the Japanese gentleman had finished his soup, the Texan asked him "Likee soupee?" The Japanese man nodded. Throughout the meal the American asked such questions as: "Likee fishee?" or "Likee drinkee?" When the meal was finished the chairman introduced the Japanese as the guest speaker of the meeting. The Japanese gentleman gave a witty speech in perfect English. After his speech he returned to his seat and asked the Texan, "Likee speechee?"

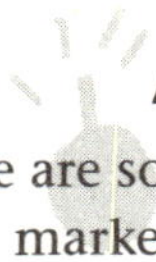

ATTENTION, PLEASE!

There are some things to improve in the dialogues. We've marked them in *italics*. Can you correct them?

Putting one's foot in it

Uwe Tissmann is very interested in meeting as many people as possible to get to know the culture of the company and its employees. Of course, there are also other foreigners in the company. Here are a couple of scenes from the Tissmann book of experience.

Mr Kowakawi (K) from Japan has an appointment with Tissmann (T). He is interested in co-operation with MEDIQUIP in Germany and wants to know more about the wheelchair range. Dr Tissmann is explaining the features.

T: (fade in) and so we developed some features which we think are absolutely necessary and have to be included on a wheelchair for a normal user in the city. By the way, the rules set by the government are very strict.
K: Yes, we have an *equal* situation in Japan. More rules every day. That is life nowadays.
T: Terrible! So it's the same in Japan. Okay, let me describe the vehicle. First feature is ... (fade out)
... and that means that the wheelchair user is able to climb *safe* onto the pavement. We call it the 'Balancer'. Excuse me, Mr Kowakawi. Well, I'm speechless ... are you asleep, Mr Kowakawi? Sorry, *if I bore* you with my ...
K: Quite to the contrary, Dr Tissmann! Very interesting, your 'Balancer'.
T: Well, really?

MEDIMAKE has an agency in Saudi Arabia and Mr. Alu Dubi (D) is in Nottingham to visit headquarters. After work Tissmann and Alex Shamcock (S) are talking to him in the bar of the Victoria Hotel.

D: (fade in) ... so that we feel that there is a large potential growth in Saudi. And, in general, you can say there's money enough for these investments in health.
S: Yes, I believe there's a high standard of living in the whole region.
T: Yes, indeed, I *have visited* the Persian Gulf last year and I was very impressed.

D: The Persian Gulf?

T: Yes, Mr Dubi. By the way; you know I *stay* here at this hotel and I've found something very special. A genuine Western Isles of Scotland whisky. It's extra special. We don't *become* anything like that on the Continent.

S: Yes, those whiskies are special. They don't export them.

T: Please be my guest. Do try this whisky.

D: Thank you, Dr Tissmann, but I'm afraid I can't drink any alcohol.

T: Come on, Mr Alu Dubi, the taste of this is so perfect, it's *heavy* to refuse it. It tastes of the turf. I ...

D: (interrupting). Gentlemen, it's very kind of you. I may not and will not drink alcohol.

S: Oh, I see. That's all no problem. What about a juice?

D: Yes please, a fresh orange juice.

T: Excellent! Here you are. Gentlemen, to international culture and understanding. Cheers!

TASK 1: Key words in business

einen Termin haben bei ...	have an ______________ with ...
an einer Zusammenarbeit mit ... interessiert sein	be interested _____ _________ with
neue Funktionen entwickeln	______________ new features
das Fahrzeug beschreiben	describe the ______________
Die Vorschriften der Regierung sind streng.	The rules _________ ___ the government are strict.
große Wachstumschancen	large potential ______________

Time for a smile

"Any alcohol?" demands the Saudi customs official.
"No, thanks," answered Klaus, "I've got enough in my suitcase."

TASK 2: Pitfalls for Germans

Could you correct these mistakes?

Grammar

1. The wheelchair user is able to climb *safe* onto the pavement.
2. Sorry, *if I bore* you with my ...? (➔ See Task 6)
3. I stay here at this hotel. (➔ See Task 6)
4. I *have visited* the Persian Gulf last year.

Vocabulary

5. We don't *become* anything like that in Germany. (➔ See Task 5A)
6. Yes, we have an *equal* situation in Japan. (➔ See Task 5B)
7. It's *heavy* to refuse this whisky. (➔ See Task 5)

TASK 3: Cross-cultural mistakes

Why should Tissmann not have said ...?

1. Well, ... are you asleep, Mr Kowakawi?
2. I visited the Persian Gulf last year.
3. Please be my guest. Do try this whisky!

TASK 4: Joke your way round trouble spots

Become ist nicht bekommen!

A German customer asks: "Can I become an egg?" The assistant said laughing, "I don't know if you can, but if you do, I'll certainly boil you. It's part of the service."

werden	get
	grow (langsam)
	go
	become

become, go, get, grow – you decide

1. The young man asked the beautiful girl to marry him. He mentioned that his father was 98 and very rich.
   She ______________ his step-mother.
2. "You can't resign," said the circus manager to the human cannonball. "Where would I ______________ another man of your calibre?"
3. Do not complain about ______________ old.
   Many are denied the privilege.
4. "Doctor, I think I am ______________ mad. Every time I ask someone the time, I ______________ a different answer."
5. A Scottish Wedding:
   Guest: "I believe she is your third daughter to ______________ married, isn't she?"
   Jock: "Yes, and the confetti is ______________ dirtier each time."

TASK 5: More trouble spots to joke around

One word in German – three words in English

A. schwer	difficult
	hard
	heavy

1. Doctor, doctor! Everybody thinks I'm a liar.
   Hmmmm! I find this very ______________ to believe.
2. There are two things that are more ______________ than making an after-dinner speech: climbing a wall which is leaning toward you and kissing a girl who is leaning away from you.
3. In the museum visitors' book, under the heading "Reason for visit", someone had written: "______________ shower."
4. It's ______________ to get a man to understand something when his salary depends upon his not understanding it.

B. gleich	same
	equal
	alike

1. Teenagers express a burning desire to be different from anyone else, then dress exactly ______________ .
2. In our company all colleagues are ______________ – only the salaries aren't.
3. "That essay on the dog is exactly word for word the ____________ as your brother's." – "Of course sir, it's the ______________ dog."

TASK 6: Joking your way through grammar

1. The interior decorator installed a skylight in my apartment. The people who (*live*) above me are furious!
2. I (*live*) so far beyond my income that we may almost be said to be living apart.
3. The managing director (*leave*) a business meeting when he saw one of the company's secretaries waiting for the rain to stop. "Excuse me," he said politely, "may I take you home in my car?" – "Yes, of course," was the reply. "Where (you / *live*)?"
4. An old Indian (*observe*) his teenage daughter's party and was fascinated by the modern dances the young people (*enjoy*). Scratching his head, he said to his wife, "Well, if that doesn't bring rain, nothing will."

Time for a smile

The reason why the Arabs lost the Six Days' War was the tanks supplied by the Russians. The handbook for the tanks gave the following instructions:

1. Retreat.
2. Draw the enemy into a trap.
3. Then wait for the winter snow.

FOCUS: Japanese business etiquette

1. The basis of Japanese business etiquette is mutual trust and respect for individuals, companies and values.
2. They are highly status-conscious. Top level executives expect to do business with top level managers from the other company. It is a sign of respect. Never use first names.
3. Before a business relationship can be formed one must get to know and trust a person.
4. Before you make an appointment send detailed printed information about your company. Your Japanese partners expect you to ask for the same.
5. They do not like newcomers. Make appointments before you arrive in the country. The best way is to be introduced personally by a Japanese agent, or better by a Japanese business partner.
6. When you are introduced give them your business card. Cards are also exchanged at parties. You might need up to 30 cards a day. Your cards should be in English and Japanese. You need a qualified professional translator to get it done properly.
7. When offered a business card, do not put it in your pocket. Read it immediately and leave it in front of you on the table.
8. Japanese do not shake hands. If they offer handshakes to westerners it should be followed by a slight bow of your head. Imitate your host. The grip should be gentle.
9. When talking to Japanese keep a greater distance than at home. And do not point with your finger, it is impolite. Do not look them straight in the eyes. It is rude.
10. They enjoy making carefully chosen personal gifts. Westerners are often surprised at the trouble they take to find out about a visitor's family. Follow their example when they visit you.
11. Do not send smart Susan to get the contract. The Japanese Samurai feels uncomfortable in the presence of clever business women who try to negotiate in an aggressive way. Women are rarely invited into the men's social circles.
12. Dress conservatively: Blue or grey suit, white shirt, dark tie. They like clean, not too young, not too hairy, modest and calm people.

FOCUS: What (not) to do in Saudi Arabia

Dos

1. Work with a Saudi agent who arranges meetings and introduces you to the right persons.
2. Begin the meeting with social conversation and be prepared for many interruptions.
3. If possible choose the seat next to the most senior person. Try to win his confidence. Do a lot of talking.
4. Discuss contracts as a matter between friends. Keep your word to the letter at all times. Personal integrity is as important as facts, figures and profit.
5. Accept all invitations. Give your gift in front of others so that there will be no appearance of bribery.
6. Take only the food that is offered to you. Eat with your right hand. Leave soon after eating.
7. Avoid unpleasant subjects like accidents, poverty, death. Praise the country, its food and fashion.

Don'ts

1. Don't conduct business via mail, telephone or fax.
2. It's not a woman's country. Don't shake hands with women.
3. Don't be impatient. Meetings have no fixed beginnings or endings; don't press them for an immediate answer.
4. Don't try to finalise a deal at the first meeting.
5. Don't refer to the Gulf as the Persian Gulf. It is the Arab Gulf.
6. Don't call them Mohammedans, they are Moslems.
7. Don't enquire about the host's wives or daughters.
8. Don't discuss women, politics or religion.
9. Don't ask them to unpack a present in your presence.
10. Don't admire your host's pictures, furniture or horses. He might feel obliged to give them to you as a present.
11. Don't point the sole of the foot towards someone when seated.
12. Islamic law is the basis of all commercial and social law. Don't touch alcohol. Don't eat, drink or smoke in public during Ramadan.

MAGIC Squares

Match the sentences with the words. Put the right number in the magic squares below. All columns and rows will add up to the same number.

Notiz: is it *note, notes* or *notice*?
während: is it *during* or *while*?
wenig: *little* or *less*
seit: is it *for* or *since*?

1. notice	**2.** while	**3.** since
4. during	**5.** notes	**6.** for
7. less	**8.** note	**9.** little

A. A man bought a parrot at an auction after some very brisk bidding. "I hope this bird talks," he said to the auctioneer. "Does he talk? Who do you think has been bidding against you ___ the past twenty minutes?"

B. How not to give ___ to your employee: "Dobson," said the boss one morning, "I just don't know how we are going to get along without you – but starting Monday, we're going to try."

C. My bank just sent me a ___ that my account is overdrawn again. I'm going to try another bank. They can't all be overdrawn.

D. McGregor was so mean he used to heat the knives so the family would use ___ butter.

E. The guest speaker was nervously studying the ___ for his speech when the chairman walked up to him and asked, "Are you ready to speak, sir? Or shall we allow them to enjoy themselves a little longer?"

F. I said to my son, "Finish up all your meat, and you'll grow up to be just like Daddy." ___ then he only has eaten vegetables.

G. No woman has ever shot her husband ___ he was doing the dishes.

H. Teacher: I wish you would pay a ___ attention.
Student: But I'm paying as ___ as I can.

I. ___ the dance the blonde says to her partner, "I'm dancing a tango, and you?"

A =	B =	C =
D =	E =	F =
G =	H =	I =

Double check

Now you will be able to master these problems:

Notizen machen	take ________________
einen Brief erhalten	receive a ____________
kündigen	give ________________
seit zwei Stunden	____________ two hours
seit damals	____________ then
weniger Geld	____________ money
wenig Erfolg	____________ success
während wir arbeiteten	____________ we were working
während der Arbeitszeit	____________ working hours

WORD AID

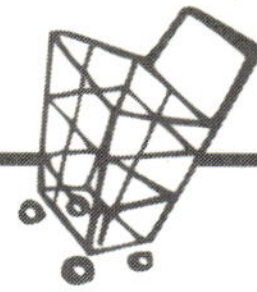

attitude	*Einstellung, Haltung*
bid	*bieten*
boil	*sieden; kochen*
border	*Grenze*
bore	*langweilen; Langweiler*
bow	*Verbeugung; sich verbeugen*
bribery	*Bestechung*
brisk	*schnell, lebhaft*
confidence	*Vertrauen*
contrary	*Gegenteil*
demand	*fragen; fordern*
deny someone something	*jemandem etwas vorenthalten, nicht gönnen*
depend upon	*ahängen von*
desire	*Wunsch*
distance	*Abstand*
essay	*Aufsatz*
furious	*wütend*
genuine	*echt*
gift	*Geschenk; Gabe*
growth	*Wachstum*
habit	*Gewohnheit*
host	*Gastgeber*
impolite	*unhöflich*
impressed	*beeindruckt*
include	*einschließen, aufnehmen*
interruption	*Unterbrechung*
letter; to the ~	*auf den Buchstaben genau*
liar	*Lügner*
mean	*geizig; gemein*
mutual trust	*gegenseitiges Vertrauen*
nod	*nicken*
overdraw	*überziehen*

parrot	*Papagei*
pavement	*Gehsteig*
praise	*Lob*
put one's foot in it	*ins Fettnäpfchen treten*
refuse	*sich weigern; ablehnen*
resign	*zurücktreten; ausscheiden*
retreat	*sich zurückziehen*
rude	*unhöflich*
senior person	*ältere Person*
skylight	*Deckenfenster*
smart	*clever; gerissen*
status-conscious	*statusbewusst*
step-mother	*Stiefmutter*
suitcase	*Koffer*
tie	*Krawatte*
translator	*Übersetzer*
trap	*Falle*
user	*Benutzer*
vehicle	*Gefährt, Fahrzeug*
witty speech	*geistreiche Rede*

SHOWING VISITORS AROUND*

Chapter 15

English is a large field with many different areas of language including the terminology of technology, medicine, economics, management, education etc. etc. One area is general business English and communication within companies. The whole thing is made more complicated by the vocabulary used in the various departments – purchasing, sales, personnel and the like. With all this in mind it is worth compiling one's own dictionary.

Time for a smile

A group of German tourists make their way to the top of Mount Etna and look into the smoke-filled crater. One of them turns to his neighbour and says, "It looks just like hell."
The Italian guide hears this, shakes his head and mutters, "Oh, these Germans! They've been everywhere!"

ATTENTION, PLEASE!

There are some things to improve in the text.
We've marked them in *italics*. Can you correct them?

* Wortschatz rund um die Firma lernen und üben Sie in Satzbeispielen mit *Build up Your Word Power. Wortschatztraining on the Job*, rororo sprachen.

A guided tour of the plant

One of the briefs that Dr Tissmann received from the Board in Germany was to do a benchmarking concerning the overall organisation of the plant. With this in mind he arranged to be taken on a tour of the major departments by a representative from the PR department. John Edwards (E) and Uwe Tissmann (T) on a personal tour.

E: I must tell you it's a real pleasure to be able to take you round the plant.

T: Yes, I've eagerly been waiting for the chance, too. It was very difficult to fix a *date* with you.

E: Sorry about that. It's a busy time. If it's okay with you I thought I'd show you round the offices first and then go out to the assembly hall and workshops.

T: Fine, where shall we start?

E: Let's go into the reception area where Mrs Smith sits. Into the lift and up to the sixth floor. We have only six levels here in total. Here on the first floor is the purchasing. As you see about fifteen people take care of a purchasing volume of £6 million.

T: They *earn* a *price* for the work they do. What's your approach on make or buy?

E: That's a hot potato. Two years ago all the talk was outsourcing. It's cheaper to get everything assembled outside. Since then we've seen that there are problems with quality.

T: And that means extra costs again. It doesn't *spare* money at all.

E: Through the double glass doors is the sales and marketing comprising a staff of twenty-five. Our six product lines are shared out amongst these employees. These teams are the sales support for the field sales staff.

T: Yes, I *have been* out helping to sell with one of them two weeks ago (fade out)

T: I'm very impressed with our automatic assembly lines. The whole thing is highly sophisticated especially with these plastic parts. I suppose you get a lot of *damages* with components like these.

E: No, it's the other way round. If anything goes wrong and a user is injured, we have to pay compensation.

T: No, no! We're talking *past each other*. I mean the plastic components can easily be broken or damaged. Can you describe what your quality control procedures are?

E: Certainly. Just over here you can see ... (fade out).

TASK 1: Key words in business

über die Sachlage informiert werden	___________ a brief
einen Termin vereinbaren	___________ an appointment
ein Einkaufsvolumen von 6 Millionen Pfund	a ___________ ___________ of £6 million
Was ist Ihre Einstellung zum Thema Eigenproduktion oder Zukauf?	What's your approach on _______ or buy?
Das ist ein heißes Eisen.	That's a ________ ___________ .
alles außerhalb montieren lassen	get everything _________ outside
Sechs Produktreihen sind auf drei Teams verteilt.	Six product lines are ___________ ___________ amongst three teams.
der Innendienst für die Verkäufer im Außendienst	the sales support for the ________ staff
Schadenersatz zahlen müssen	have to pay ___________

TASK 2: Pitfalls for Germans

Could you correct these mistakes? (See also Task 4)

1. It was very difficult to fix a *date* with you.
2. They *earn* a *price* for the work they do.
3. It doesn't *spare* money at all.
4. We're talking *past each other.*
5. I suppose you get a lot of *damages* with components like these.
6. I *have been* out helping to sell with one of them two weeks ago.

TASK 3: Test your memory

	True	False
1. First, they visited the assembly hall and workshops.		✔
2. The purchasing department is on the sixth floor.		
3. About fifteen people sell goods for £6 million.		
4. They don't outsource any more.		
5. Six product lines are shared out amongst 25 employees.		

TASK 4: Joke your way round trouble spots

verdienen – is it *earn* or *deserve*?

1. Democracy is a system that ensures that we shall be governed no better than we (*verdienen*). G.B. SHAW
2. The income tax authorities have made up a new tax form with only two lines:
   1. How much do you (*verdienen*)?
   2. Send it.

Preis – is it *price* or *prize*?

1. It's terrible bringing up a family today, considering the (*Preis*) of beer and cigarettes. WOODY ALLEN
2. Steve Helms has been awarded the first (*Preis*) for the best salesman of the year. He sold two milking machines to a farmer with one cow, and took the cow as a down payment.
3. How do you double the (*Preis*) of a Trabbi? Fill up the petrol tank.

Let's double check it:

An ideal response from the guest of honour.
"I really don't (*verdienen*) this (*Preis*). But then, I've got arthritis and I didn't (*verdienen*) that either."

Verabredung, Termin –
is it *date, deadline* or *appointment*?

1. I had an (*Verabredung*) with my doctor this morning. He gave me six months to live, but when I couldn't pay the bill he gave me six months more. WALTER MATTHAU
2. All successful advertising campaigns which target men include one of these three messages:
   A. This product will help you get (*Verabredungen*) with bikini models.
   B. This product will save you time and money, which you'll need if you want (*sich verabreden mit*) bikini models.
   In order to appeal to women's greater range of intellectual interests specifically, your message has to say this:
   C. If you buy this product, you'll look like a bikini model. SCOTT ADAMS
3. Can we fix a (*Termin*) for the next meeting?
4. I'd better get a move on – next week is the (*Termin*) for handing in my application.

Is it *damage* or *damages*?

1. The storm had caused some ________________ .
2. He sued the company and won £5,000 (in) ______________ .
3. If there is a possibility of several things going wrong, the one that will cause the most ______________will be the one to go wrong.

PHRASES Master your phrases: Looking around the company

Ich glaube, ich sollte Ihnen etwas über unsere Firma erzählen.	I think I ought to tell you something about the company.
Die Firma wurde 1960 gegründet.	The company was founded in 1960.
Wir sind einer der führenden Lieferanten von medizinischen Geräten.	We are one of the leading suppliers of medical equipment.
Wir sind hauptsächlich auf zahntechnischem Gebiet tätig.	Our principal operations are in the dental sector.
Unsere Produktionsstätte befindet sich auf dem Firmengelände.	Our production facility is on site.
Hier sehen Sie ...	Here you can see ...
Hier fertigen / produzieren wir ...	This is where we produce ...
Das Gebäude da drüben ist ...	That building over there is ...
Vor uns sehen Sie ...	In front of us you can see ...
Neben dem Lager befindet sich die Forschungsabteilung.	Next to the warehouse there is the research department.
Leider dürfen wir da nicht rein.	I'm afraid we can't go in there.
Man darf hier nicht fotografieren / keine Fotos machen.	You can't take photos in there.
Handys sind in diesem Gebäude nicht erlaubt.	Mobile phones (cell phones) are forbidden in this building.
Gegenüber ist der Fuhrpark.	Opposite there is the transport pool.
Wir müssen in der Montagehalle unsere (Schutz-)Helme aufsetzen.	We have to wear our helmets in the assembly plant.
Dies ist eine Nichtraucherzone.	This is a no-smoking area.

Time for a smile

He has a problem about the future. He's getting married in a month and he hasn't found a job for his wife.

TASK 5: More trouble spots to joke around

One word in German – two words in English

tragen	carry
	wear

1. We have to __________ our helmets in the assembly plant.
2. "Do you sell pillow cases?"
   "Yes, Sir. What size do you need?"
   "I really don't know, but I __________ a size seven hat."
3. Our modern world is so full of problems that if Moses came down from Mount Sinai again, the two tablets he'd be __________ would be aspirins.
4. I put the wrong size of battery in the beeper that I __________ on my belt. The first call I got blew my shoes off.
5. Fashion is what one __________ oneself. What is unfashionable is what other people __________. OSCAR WILDE
6. Three Scotsmen were visiting London for a holiday and on Sunday they went to church. As the collection plate moved closer, they became more and more worried. Just before the plate reached them, one of the Scotsmen fainted and the other two __________ him out of the church.

Time for a smile

Guide on a conducted tour of Rome: "And this ancient monument dates back over 2000 years."
"Don't be ridiculous," said one little old lady. "It's only 1990 now."

TASK 6: A quiz on the company

The guide explains, but do you know where you are?
The first one has been done for you.

1. The gentleman here will check our passes. Main gate
2. These young ladies welcome our visitors and show them to the right room. ____________
3. On our right we can have a tea or coffee. ____________
4. Over there we store the finished products. ____________
5. Here you can see how the components are put together. ____________
6. The company cars are over there. One of our chauffeurs will drive you back to the station. ____________
7. My colleagues here are on the look out for new products and new markets. ____________
8. The gentlemen in this building are responsible for innovation. ____________
9. The chaps on the third floor watch over the budgets. ____________
10. On the second floor they buy the components for the scales. ____________
11. Through the glass door you can watch the guys who try to get rid of our products. ____________
12. These people tell customers how good our products are. ____________
13. They know how to handle the angry customers and their problems. ____________
14. Those people in uniforms watch over our safety and security day and night. ____________
15. And these charming young ladies provide us with stationery and sometimes type our papers. ____________
16. These gentlemen sit at expensive desks at the carpet level and smoke Havannas. ____________
17. This charming smart lady is the workhorse of the company. She organises the boss. ____________

WORD AID

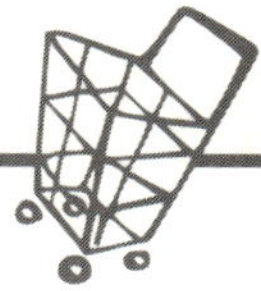

approach	*Methode*
assemble	*montieren, zusammenbauen*
assembly hall	*Montagehalle*
assembly line	*Montageband*
awarded; be ~ a prize	*einen Preis erhalten*
compensation; pay ~	*Schadenersatz leisten*
compile	*sammeln, zusammenstellen*
component	*Bauteil*
comprise	*umfassen*
control procedures	*Kontrollverfahren*
down payment	*Anzahlung*
economics	*Wirtschaftswissenschaften*
ensure	*gewährleisten, sicherstellen*
faint	*ohnmächtig werden*
field sales staff	*Verkaufspersonal im Außendienst*
move; get a ~ on	*sich beeilen*
mutter	*murmeln*
pillow case	*Kopfkissenbezug*
purchasing	*Einkaufsabteilung*
response	*Antwort*
sales support	*Verkaufspersonal im Innendienst*
shake	*schütteln; zittern*
share out among	*aufteilen unter*
size seven	*Größe sieben*
sophisticated	*hoch entwickelt, kompliziert*
stationery	*Büromaterial*
subject	*Gegenstand, Thema*
sue someone	*jemanden verklagen*
tablet	*Tablette; Tafel*
target	*Ziel; sich richten an*
various	*verschieden(e)*
workshop	*Werkstatt*

16 Chapter

DISCUSSING THE MERGER

The world of business is changing rapidly. It's not enough nowadays to be good at your job, for your company to be good at its job. Today we are all part of a great game of Monopoly. Companies are bought and sold for various reasons. It can be to complement the buyer's range with products he does not offer, to create a more powerful presence on the market by combining the turnovers of two companies, or to destroy the acquired company by selling parts of it off. One competitor less! But what does all this mean for the staff? It normally accompanies fears of job losses, dissatisfaction and demotivation. And probably unemployment!

How to motivate the staff

It's going to be a very tough year.
Don't expect much in terms of raises. Work should be its own reward.
If we don't make more profit next year, we'll have more layoffs.
Actually, we'll probably have more layoffs anyway.
Scott Adams, The Dilbert Principle

ATTENTION, PLEASE!

There are eight things to improve in the text.
We've marked them in *italics.* Can you correct them?

Fears of wasting away

Tissmann has had some pleasant and some not so pleasant meetings on the island. There had been misunderstandings, but most problems were solved in an amicable way. Unfortunately the same could not be said of the meeting with the trade union representative. As if things were not bad enough, and now this meeting and it was official in some way. Tissmann had better be careful what he says. Tissmann (**T**), Bloggs (**B**), the union man, Peter Long (**L**), Head of Personnel.

B: (fade in) ... so I'm really glad after all this time to have finally got a meeting with you.

L: I assure you, Mr Bloggs, that Dr Tissmann has had a very busy schedule.

B: I'm sure he has. It's just a pity that he couldn't find time to talk to the workforce, the greatest asset of any company. You wouldn't be where you are, Mr Long, without us.

T: My dear Mr Bloggs. Let's try to listen to each other. I'm certain we can meet each other halfway.

B: Let's hope so! Look, I'll come straight to the point. MEDIQUIP has more or less bought us out at MEDIMAKE. You offer many very similar lines. That means parallel work. People doing the same jobs. And we all know where that'll end up. Job losses! How many men are going to be fired?

T: Of course, I understand your nervousness concerning your members ...

B: (interrupting) Concerning our workforce to be precise, not only our members.

T: Yes, yes, of course. It is clear to me that you are very *engaged for* the workforce. And I am the first person to say that this is a very *uncomfortable* situation.

B: Well, that's a classical understatement, if I may say so.

T: Firstly, we don't want to fire people ad hoc. In many cases when a worker retires his job may not be filled. We call this natural wastage. Some of your *personal* will leave the company. They will not be replaced. In this way we can get our numbers down.

B: Well, that's a fine thing to say about your superfluous staff! I don't believe for a minute that you can solve all your problems like that.

Look, give us an idea of how the changes are going to affect us. We have a right to know.

T: Mr Bloggs, I am not the responsible person to say what our Board of Management intends. What I can say is that this *fusion* is in the best interests of both companies. Have you thought that workers in Germany can also lose their jobs? We are all *sitting* in *one* boat. We must pull together.

L: I couldn't have put it better myself, Dr Tissmann.

B: I'm afraid I'm still not convinced, Mr Tissmann. I'd like statements, solutions, plans. The truth!

T: I understand what you're saying. You know just *so good as* I that there are no *receipts* for every situation. We have to accept that fact. I cannot *underwrite* a sheet of paper which promises you things I cannot implement. As for... (fade out)

TASK 1: Key words in business

eine Produktreihe ergänzen	____________ a product range
die Umsätze zweier Firmen vereinen	__________ the ____________ of two companies
Vertreter der Gewerkschaft	_______ ______ representatives
einen vollen Terminkalender haben	have a very ____________ schedule
Das Personal ist der größte Vermögensposten einer Firma.	The staff is the greatest ____________ of a company.
Wir nennen es natürliche Abgänge.	We call it _________________ _______________.
Die Veränderungen werden sich auf uns auswirken.	The changes are going to ____________ us.

Time for a smile

Can you imagine the whole world
being created in six days and six nights?
Fortunately we now have the trade unions.

TASK 2: Pitfalls for Germans

Could you correct these mistakes?

Tricky words

1. What I can say is that this *fusion* is in the best interests of both companies.
2. There are no *receipts* for every situation ...
3. And I am the first person to say that this is a very *uncomfortable* situation.
4. It is clear to me that you are very *engaged for* the workforce.
5. I cannot *underwrite* a sheet of paper which promises you things I cannot implement.
6. Some of your *personal* will leave the company.

Tricky Grammar

7. We *are* all *sitting* in *one* boat.
8. You know *so* good *as* I that ...

TASK 3: Test your memory

1. Why did Tissmann not meet Bloggs earlier?
2. Why is Bloggs afraid of parallel work?
3. What does Tissmann understand by 'natural wastage'?

TASK 4: Beef up your word power

Find the opposite.

set on new staff	______________________ off staff
hire workers	______________________ workers
employ a secretary	______________________ a secretary

TASK 5: Joke your way round trouble spots

Which words fit into the jokes?
Sometimes there is more than one solution.

1. An applicant was interviewed for a vacancy. "What we are looking for," said the personnel manager, "is a man with energy, ____________ and courage, a man who can inspire others, in short a man who can pull the company's football team up from the bottom of the league."

A. engagement **B.** dedication **C.** commitment

2. "Dear John
I have been unable to sleep since I broke off our ____________.
Won't you forget and forgive? Your absence is breaking my heart. I was a fool, nobody can take your place. I love you; I love you.
Mary
PS: Congratulations on winning the lottery."

A. engagement **B.** wedding **C.** marriage

3. Bell invented the telephone, but he found it was useless until he invented the second telephone. This was fine, until he invented the third telephone. He phoned the second, and found it __________.

A. engaged **B.** occupied **C.** committed

4. The company has been expanding on the home market, so the boss invited his sales team into his office. "You have done so well that I'm giving you all a cheque for $1,500," he said – and on second thoughts he added, "and if you keep on working like this, I might even ____________________ them."

A. underwrite **B.** sign **C.** signature

5. An insurance broker had just tied up a big deal with the boss of a chemical plant, agreeing to ____________ a policy to insure his warehouse for a large sum. As he signed the contract, the businessman asked jokingly, "And what do I get if the place burns down tonight?" – "At least ten years," said the insurance broker.

A. underwrite **B.** sign **C.** authorized

TASK 6: More pitfalls to joke around

Which words fit best?
Sometimes there is more than one solution.

1. A personnel manager found himself in an ____________ situation. A month before, he had agreed to employ a new worker, but by the time the man arrived for his first day they had reorganised the company and the position he had intended to fill had disappeared. "Oh, don't worry," said the new employee, quite unconcerned. "The little bit of work I do won't be noticed by anybody."

   A. unpleasant **B.** embarrassing **C.** uncomfortable

2. The managing director was looking over the expense accounts of the purchasing department. – "What are these ____________ here?" he asked his purchasing manager. "They seem a bit excessive." – "Oh, those are our restaurant bills." – "Well, in future," said the managing director, "don't buy any more restaurants."

   A. prescriptions **B.** recipe **C.** receipts

3. Finally, I've been asked by the organisers to announce that, for reasons of safety, at the end of this talk you are requested to refrain from getting up on to the tables or chairs during my standing ovation. Thank you for your ____________.

   A. prescriptions **B.** co-operation **C.** understanding

4. An Englishman is a creature who thinks he is being moral when he is only being ____________ G. MIKES

   A. unpleasant **B.** uncomfortable **C.** embarrassing

5. During a meeting the chairman said to the young manager, "Your ____________ contains a lot of new and good ideas. However, the good ideas aren't new, and the new ideas aren't good."

   A. contribution **B.** collaboration **C.** co-operation

6. Ronny told Annette that there was a chance that radiation caused by nuclear ____________ might hurt his reproductive organs, but she said in her opinion it was a small price to pay.

A. fusion **B.** fission **C.** merger

7. Many years ago, when the Pepsi-Cola Company was in terrible financial trouble, Coca-Cola was offered the chance of buying them out. They figured that Pepsi couldn't last long anyway and turned down the opportunity of a ____________. Now Pepsi and Coke are arch-rivals and have an almost equal share in the world market.

A. merger **B.** takeover **C.** fusion

TASK 7: Two more tricky words

Is it *personnel* or *personal*?

"Can you do shorthand?" asked the __________ Manager.
"Yes, but it takes me longer," answered the young secretary.

When the boss came into the office fifteen minutes early one morning, he surprised the office manager locked in fond embrace with his ____________ assistant. "Dobson!" thundered the boss, "You're not paid to do this, you know!"
"I know, sir," replied Dobson. "But I don't mind."

FOCUS: The union's fight for job security

Well, we saw that Tissmann had his problems with old Bloggs. In the old days the trade unions used to be more powerful than they are now. It took a decade of Mrs Thatcher to break their power, now their influence is more limited. However, they still have their role to play. The *trade union representative* tries his best to represent the interests of the workers and even the office staff. It could be the shop steward who discusses the *items* mentioned above. These fighters for workers' rights are best known for their *attempts* to get wages *raised* every year. And, of course, they are the officials who call the men out on strike (unless it's a *wild cat strike*). The trade union representative is paid for the time he spends on work in industrial relations in England.
What sort of things did the unions fight for? Here are a few examples.

trade union representative	*Vertreter der Gewerkschaft*
items	*Thema*
attempts	*Versuch*
raised	*erhöhen*
wild cat strike	*wilder Streik*

Legislation

First, what sorts of laws are in place regarding work and workers? Well, there's the *Employment Protection Act*, 1992 and the Trade Union Reform and Employment Rights Act of 1993. In the last *Act* workers get a lot more rights. For example, it includes *part-time* workers who were not covered earlier. What does this act of 1993 mean for trade unions? What did they *achieve*?

Legislation	*Gesetzgebung*
Employment Protection Act	*Gesetz zum Schutz des Arbeitsplatzes*
Act	*Gesetz*
part-time	*Teilzeit*
achieve	*erreichen*

Rules of employment?

Nowadays *maternity rights* are included, as well as the right to receive the written details on any employment. The worker also has a right to an *itemised pay statement*, so he can see how his pay cheque was arrived at. He can also use the *industrial tribunal*. These courts *set up* around the country deal with employment *disputes*

maternity rights	*Mutterschutz*
itemised pay statement	*detaillierte Lohnabrechnung*
industrial tribunal; set up; disputes	*Arbeitsgericht; einrichten; Streit*

concerning *redundancy*, equal pay and complaints for unfair *dismissal*.

Entlassung
Entlassung

The contract

Most people want a *contract of employment*. The employee *provides* the work and the employer pays him a *wage* or a *salary* for it. The contract should include the names of the employer and the employee, dates of *commencement*, rate of *remuneration* and when it is to be paid, hours of work, holiday entitlement, sickness *entitlement*, pensions, *period of notice*. And, of course, a description of the job.
It's great having security, isn't it?

Arbeitsvertrag
liefern
Lohn; Gehalt
Beginn;
Entlohnung
Anspruch;
Kündigungsfrist

WORD AID

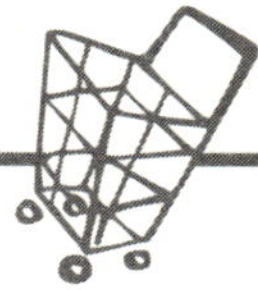

acquire a company	*eine Firma erwerben*
affect someone	*jemanden treffen, beeinträchtigen*
amicable	*freundschaftlich*
applicant	*Bewerber*
assets	*Vorteile / Aktiva*
bottom of the league	*letzter Tabellenplatz*
committed	*engagiert*
competitor	*Konkurrent*
complement a range	*eine Produktreihe ergänzen*
contain	*enthalten*
convince	*überzeugen*
destroy	*zerstören*
embarrassing	*peinlich*
expense account	*Spesenrechnung*
fond embrace	*innige Umarmung*
implement	*umsetzen, verwirklichen*
insurance broker	*Versicherungsmakler*
insure	*versichern*
layoffs	*Entlassungen*
loss	*Verlust*
parallel work	*doppelte Arbeit*
pity; it's a ~	*es ist schade*
plant	*Fabrik, Werk*
policy	*Versicherungspolice*
prescription	*Rezept (Arzt)*
pull together	*an einem Strang ziehen*
radiation	*Strahlung*
receipt	*Quittung, Beleg*
refrain from doing something	*etwas nicht tun*
reproductive organ	*Fortpflanzungsorgan*
request	*bitten*
retire	*in Pension gehen*
schedule; a busy ~	*ein voller Terminkalender*

shorthand	*Stenographie*
straight; come ~ to the point	*gleich zur Sache kommen*
superfluous staff	*nicht benötigtes Personal*
tie up a big deal	*ein großes Geschäft abschließen*
tough	*hart, zäh*
trade union	*Gewerkschaft*
truth	*Wahrheit*
uncomfortable	*ungemütlich*
underwrite	*rückversichern*
unpleasant	*unangenehm*
useless	*nutzlos*
vacancy	*freie Stelle*
waste away	*schwinden*

Chapter 17

SMALL TALK AND NETWORKS*

Some people live in the delusion that if a fellow works hard he will do well in his career. Actually, it's more likely to have the opposite effect if somebody works harder than his colleagues. People will be jealous or angry with him for rocking the boat. No, it's far more important to have the skills of small-talking and networking. This is all about the ability to get into conversation with somebody, keeping his interest, letting him talk and creating a contact that might be mutually useful later.

Time for a smile

James Peabody, director of a company in the Midlands, welcomed an important customer from Germany. "We're so pleased to have you with us. I do hope you'll enjoy your stay. On Monday night you'll be my guest at the club. You'll meet a lot of interesting people and there's a lot of drinking and ..."
"I'm sorry, sir," interrupted the German, "I don't drink."
"Oh really? Let me see. Tuesday night. We always have a dance. There are lots of pretty girls. You'll really enjoy that." "No, sir," said the German. "I don't go in for that sort of thing."
"Really? Hmm ... excuse me if I'm being indiscreet. Are you homosexual?" asked Peabody.
"Certainly not, sir."
"What a pity! In that case you won't enjoy Friday night either."

ATTENTION, PLEASE!

There are some things to improve in the dialogue. We've marked them in *italics*. Can you correct them?

Golf and business

Tissmann's time in England is nearly up. All in all it has been a good experience. He collected a lot of information, even solved a few problems. He picked up a few English habits like playing golf with the boss, Andrew Dobson (D), CEO of MEDIMAKE, which is what he's doing now.

D: I will certainly miss playing these nine holes with you when you go back to Germany.

T: *I also. As* I was living in Germany I never ever played golf.

D: Why was that? You've got a good swing.

T: Oh, *by us* it's much too expensive and there aren't enough courses. Speaking of courses, this one's lovely, isn't it?

D: Yes, green all round, rolling fields and the sun's shining, but not too strongly. I could stay here all day, but unfortunately work is calling.

T: That's right. By the way, thanks for the copy of this fiscal year's *balance* that you sent me. They'll need that back in Germany.

D: My pleasure.

T: And I'll certainly suggest to the Board *to send* 2000 of the Pulsometers to your purchasing department at the new inter-company transfer price.

D: That's fine. We'll look forward to that.

T: It's a perfect opportunity when *the course* of the *Euro* to the pound is so low.

D: Well, we need all the support we can get with our results being so weak at present.

T: I'm sure you'll soon be *writing black figures* again. MEDIMAKE's problem has certainly been blown up by the strength of the pound. No wonder that exports are down. Everything is too expensive.

D: That was a good shot. You should keep up your golf.

T: Well, actually, I was thinking of *making holiday* in Portugal at a golf hotel. That could really improve my game.

D: Portugal? What a great idea! That puts me in mind of a wonderful four weeks I once spent touring around in my camping bus ... (fade out)

TASK 1: Pitfalls for Germans

Tricky grammar

1. *I also.*
2. I'll certainly suggest to the Board *to send* 2000 of the Pulsometers.

Tricky phrases

3. *As* I was living in Germany I never ever played golf.
4. Oh, *by us* it's much too expensive.
5. Thanks for the copy of this fiscal year's *balance* that you sent me.
6. The *course* of the *Euro* to the pound is so low.
7. I'm sure you'll soon be *writing black figures* again.
8. Well, actually I was thinking of *making holiday* in Portugal at a golf hotel.

TASK 2: Joke your way round trouble spots

One word in German – four alternatives in English.
Often the place in the sentence decides which to choose.

auch	as well
	too
	also
	so ...

1. After the wedding, the bride' s dad took a taxi to the bankruptcy court. Getting out he said to the driver, "You might as well come, __________."
2. They had pollution in the old days, ___________ , but at least you could put it on your roses.
3. Of course behaviourism works. ___________ does torture. W. H. AUDEN
4. Overheard in Spaceship Enterprise approaching the Planet of Amazons: "Beam me down, Scotty. ... Very funny, Scotty! Now beam down my clothes ____________."
5. Sign in a school: "Hooks are for teachers only." Underneath, some bright spark had added: "They may ____________ be used for hats and coats."
6. Sign in a shop window: Our clothes not only make girls slim, they ____________ make men look round.

TASK 3: More trouble spots to joke around

***Rate* isn't *rate* and *course* is not always *Kurs*.**

1. An American tourist in Heidelberg sees a tramp and throws him a dollar. The tramp shouts to his tramp colleague: "Hey, Fritz, do we still take dollars at today's ________________ ?"
2. John Smith was a second ________________ author. Only three copies of his novel 'The Vampire of Alcatraz Prison' had been sold in the first six months. But one day he had a brilliant idea. He placed the following ad in several newspapers: "MILLIONAIRE, 65, GOOD-LOOKING, WISHES TO MARRY A GIRL LIKE THE HEROINE IN THE NOVEL 'THE VAMPIRE OF ALCATRAZ' by John Smith." The book was sold out within a week.
3. Insurance: paying for catastrophes on the ______________ plan.
4. One Saturday afternoon, there was a commotion on the golf ________________ as a young lady dressed in a resplendent wedding-gown stormed onto the green, walked over to a young golfer and screamed, "You miserable, no-good bastard! Do you know what day it is?" The young golfer looked up from his putt and said, "But Sylvia, I told you – only if it was raining!"
5. John, having completed a ________________ of analysis with his psychiatrist, said to his friend: "I always thought I was indecisive."
   Friend: "And now?"
   John: "I'm not so sure."
6. What they write to you ...
   "We're investigating the matter and will advise you in due ________________ ."
   ... and what it actually means:
   We can't find your correspondence.

MAGIC Squares

Match the sentences with the words. Put the right number in the magic squares below. All columns and rows will add up to the same number.

1. sheet	**2.** decision	**3.** power
4. strike	**5.** budgets	**6.** bank
7. tipped	**8.** payments	**9.** trade

A. The *balance* of ___ is the difference between the amount paid to foreign countries for imports and services and the amount received from them for exports in a given period.

B. The *balance* ___ is a written record of money received and paid out, showing the difference between the two total amounts.

C. My ___ *balance* is always low at the end of the month.

D. The three branches of the government ensure a *balance* of ___.

E. It's the task of the accountants to balance the ___.

F. Her greater experience ___ the *balance* in her favour. She got the job.

G. It was difficult to ___ the right *balance* between justice and necessity.

H. *Balance* of ___ is the difference in value between exports and imports.

I. After comparing all the arguments they reached a *balanced* ___.

A =	**B =**	**C =**
D =	**E =**	**F =**
G =	**H =**	**I =**

FOCUS: Three levels of small talk

First: **Small talk without a purpose**

There are three levels of small talk. The first is small talk pure, innocent small talk without any thought of how to profit by it professionally. It is small talk without a purpose. If you are a good small talker on the first level you are a 'Four-E-Expert' because you

1. enjoy the moment and the company,
2. encourage others to participate,
3. engage in satisfying contact with people,
4. exchange information and ideas with others.

Second: **Small talk with a purpose**

If you want to become a good small talker on the second level you will have to master the fifth E and

5. explore a new business opportunity.

Small talk is not only a social skill, but also a business skill. Business people engage in small talk with a purpose. The fifth E means creating contacts through small talk with people you are professionally interested in.

Third: **Small talk for networking**

The effective networker makes the most of his personal contacts. He is the Six-E-Expert: He wants to

6. establish a network as a bridge to professional success.

The Six-E-Expert knows that it's not important what you know, but who you know. Small talkers with a vision try to find a place in a network of partners who collect and exchange useful information over a longer period of time.

WORD AID

amount	*Summe, Betrag*
collect	*sammeln*
commotion	*Aufregung*
delusion	*Täuschung*
fiscal year	*Geschäftsjahr*
habit	*Gewohnheit*
hook	*Garderobehaken*
improve	*verbessern*
indecisive	*unentschlossen*
investigate	*untersuchen*
jealous	*eifersüchtig*
mutually useful	*zum beiderseitigen Nutzen*
participate	*teilnehmen*
pollution	*Umweltverschmutzung*
profit by	*profitieren von*
purpose	*Ziel, Zweck*
resplendent	*strahlend*
skill	*Fertigkeit*
slim	*schlank*
stay	*Aufenthalt*
support	*Unterstützung*
swing	*Schwung*
wedding	*Hochzeit*
wedding-gown	*Hochzeitskleid*

CLASSROOM ACTIVITIES

Chapter 1: All about companies. Divide in pairs. Each member of the pair should make a mini-presentation of the company he / she works for. The presentation should include the number of employees, company structure, ranges of products and markets etc.
The listener may ask questions about the company.

Chapter 2: Presenting oneself. Divide into small groups of four. One of the four is a candidate for a job. The group should decide what sort of job. Then the other three group members are the interviewing panel. The candidate should describe himself, his qualifications, his CV, etc.

Chapter 3: The business trip. Divide into pairs and play out the following situations:
a) discussion at customs
b) argument with hotel reception
c) first meeting with the managing director
d) at the lost property office.

Chapter 4: Into pairs. Build up the following role-plays:
a) visiting the doctor with an illness
b) doing business at the bank
c) getting to know somebody in the pub.

Chapter 5: Pair work. One person is the car salesman, the other a customer. Build up the role-play discussing price, age, pros and cons of the car.

Chapter 6: Pair work. One person is a policeman, the other a driver. The driver has done something wrong.

Chapter 7: Pair work. Select a type of shop. Build up the discussion between the shop assistant and the customer. Discuss price, size, variety and quality.

Chapter 8: Divide into groups of four. Build up a business meeting between Dr Tissmann and three members of the English company. Make an agenda, choose your own topics.

Chapter 9: Into pairs. Together prepare a speech congratulating somebody on something. One person starts the speech off and it is completed by the second person. You are congratulating somebody in the whole group. Invent details about that person including character, age, humour, talents, etc.

Chapter 10: At the trade fair. Into groups of three. You are at a stand of the trade fair. One person is in charge of the stand. He should describe his products and his company. The other two are customers. They should ask relevant questions including price, range, quality, deliver times.

Chapter 11: Into pairs. Choose an interesting, fairly complicated product. One of you is the salesman, one the potential customer. Plan your discussion. If you are the salesman fix the price and any special conditions. If you are the customer think about your budget, discounts etc. Then come together and play the roles.

Chapter 12: Into groups of four to role-play a meeting. Choose an important subject for a meeting, one person should keep the minutes of the meeting and you should have an agenda. One person should chair the meeting.

Chapter 13: Into pairs. Each person will make a mini-presentation of five minutes to his partner in the pair.

a) my worst holiday experience
b) my ideal profession
c) memories of school
d) the most attractive character I know.

Chapter 14: Round table discussion of about eight people. Topic: national stereotypes. Do they exist? Give examples from real life.

Chapter 15: Into pairs. Each person draws a diagram of a house he knows well, including all rooms. He/she then describes it in detail taking his listener through the house. Each person suggests what he would like to do to make it a perfect residence.

TOP 30 MISTAKES QUIZ

Here you can check if you have "bettered" your business English. Choose the correct words and phrases:

1. sensible / sensitive

It is ______________ to add in this appendix because it is useful.
My muscles are too ______________ since I strained my legs jogging.

2. at last / at least

We expected to achieve ______________ the same turnover as last year.
______________ she arrived after I'd been waiting for nearly an hour.

3. meaning / opinion

Does anybody know the ______________ of life? I'm sure I don't.
In my ______________ working in industry is a cut-throat business.

4. remember / remind

I can ______________ the good old days when summers were long and I enjoyed work.
May we ______________ you that your account is overdrawn.

5. actual / current

What's the ______________ number of products you've sold?
What's the ______________ number of employees in the company?

6. I'm working / I have been working

I ______________ at SAP for three years and I still enjoy my work.

7. attend / visit

We're going to ______________ some friends this afternoon.
She ______________ an excellent school. You can hear that when she speaks.

8. here you are / please

______________ tell me how we're going to arrive in time.
Customs official: Can I see you passport, please. Bob: Certainly.
______________ .

9. do / make

Bob: Steffi, if you don't ______________ your homework, you'll never pass your A levels.

It's been great ______________ business with you. We should do it again.

10. do / make

Jill: You're ______________ a mistake if you think you can simply lie to the boss. He's not stupid.

Ann: But I tell you I ______________ my overtime. It's not a lie.

11. used to drive / be used to driving

Bob ______________ but then he lost his licence through drink driving.

Ron ______________ at night. He has no problem with it.

12. check / control

Could you ______________ how many employees are on the payroll at present?

The general will not be able to ______________ his soldiers. They'll rebel.

13. etwas machen lassen: Which sentence has this meaning?

a) Ron has his car cleaned every week.

b) We have cleaned our car already.

14. in the near of / near to

We live in Wieblingen. Actually, it's very ______________ Heidelberg.

15. brief / short

Dear Colleagues, I know we don't have much time today, so I'd like to be ______________ .

16. defect / defective

Angry customer: This car was ______________ when I bought it. You should give me my money back.

17. prospect / prospectus

Customer: I'm very interested in your product range. Could you give me a ______________ .

18. greater / larger

Our company has become much ______________ in the last two years. Two hundred percent more turnover.

19. commission / provision
Salesman: If I sell your products what sort of ______________ will I get for it?

20. what for / what sort of
Ron fell in a pool full of sharks. ______________ stupidity was that?

21. policy / politics
It seems to me that the financial ______________ of our company is a bit shaky, to say the least.

22. declare / explain
Customer: could you please ______________ the benefits I'll get from your product.

23. bore / I'm boring
Chairman of the Board: Sorry, Ladies and Gentlemen, if I ______________ you with details of our financial problems, but ...

24. appointment / date
Applicant: I'd like to arrange ______________ with your personnel manager as soon as possible.

25. personal / personnel
Congratulations! I heard you've got the job as ______________ Manager at S.U.P.

26. engaged / occupied
I phoned you three times yesterday but your phone was always ______________ .

27. course / rate
The ______________ of the dollar to the pound sterling has decreased dramatically.

28. in the black figures / in the black
Financial director: Don't worry! We're still ______________ .

29. stationary / stationery
How can we write letters? We've absolutely no ______________ .

30. comfortable / convenient
A caller who dials the wrong number will call a second time as soon as you have returned to your living room and made yourself _______________ .

1. sensible; sensitive
2. at least; at last
3. meaning; opinion
4. remember; remind
5. current; actual
6. I have been working
7. attended; visit
8. please; here you are
9. do; doing
10. making; did
11. used to drive; is used to driving
12. check; control
13. a)
14. near to
15. brief
16. defective
17. prospectus
18. larger
19. commission
20. what sort of
21. policy
22. explain
23. I'm boring
24. appointment
25. personnel
26. engaged
27. rate
28. in the black
29. stationery
30. comfortable

KEY TO THE EXERCISES

CHAPTER 1

TASK 1: Key words in business

sich spezialisieren auf	specialise *in*
medizinische Geräte herstellen	*manufacture* medical equipment
gemeinsames Projekt	joint *venture*
in der gleichen Branche sein	be in the same *field*
die Gelegenheit, etwas zu tun	the *opportunity* to do something
auf dem Markt Fuß fassen	get a *foothold* in the market
Fachwissen austauschen	*exchange* know-how
Synergieeffekte entwickeln	*develop* synergies
ein möglicher Partner	a *potential* partner
die Voraussetzungen für eine Zusammenarbeit schaffen	*set* the scene for co-operation
Befürchtungen ausräumen	*smooth* over fears
eine engere Auswahl an Kandidaten	a *shortlist* of candidates
jemanden in die engere Auswahl für eine Stelle nehmen	shortlist somebody *for* a job

TASK 2: Test your memory

1. A merger would be an excellent opportunity for MEDIQUIP to get a foothold in the British market, at the same time exchanging know-how and perhaps developing synergies.
2. The idea of the merger or joint venture has to be sold; an envoy has to go to the UK to smooth over fears, to show advantages and to set the scene for later co-operation.
3. It should be a flexible, sensitive colleague, fluent in English and highly motivated.

TASK 3: Pitfalls for Germans

1. *at last:* endlich – passt hier nicht, deshalb
2. *at least:* wenigstens

1. *sensitive:* einfühlsam, sensibel; passt eher in unseren Text als
2. *sensible:* ist nicht sensibel, sondern vernünftig (auch reasonable)

TASK 4: Describing MEDIQUIP

MEDIQUIP is one of Germany's leading *suppliers* of medical equipment. The company *employs* over 300 people and has *subsidiaries* located in ten cities. It has become the *market leader* within 40 years. The company was *founded* in 1960 and its principal *operations* were in the orthodontic field. Since then the company has *grown* rapidly to meet the *needs* of both the dental and surgical sector. The company has always recognised the *requirements* of changing market needs and has *diversified* and *innovated* its *product range* in time. The *breakthrough* came with the microchip. The computerised pace-maker has become the company's cash cow. Believe it or not, the hearing-aids and ultrasound scanners have even caught the *attention* of various secret services and military leaders.

TASK 5: Remember the product?

hearing-aid	a small device that makes sounds louder and helps a deaf person to hear.
ultrasound scanner	a device to produce a picture of the inside of a person's body on a computer screen.
pace-maker	an electronic device placed under the skin near the heart to make the heart beat more regularly.

TASK 6: Joke your way round trouble spots

1. A disgusted husband shouted to his wife, "Won't you (A) *at least* keep the baby?"
2. Most laws seem (A) *reasonable* until policemen try to enforce them against nice people like us.
3. "Son," he said, "be *sensitive* to your customer's reactions."

CHAPTER 2

TASK 1: Key words in business

Medizin studieren	*do* a degree in medicine
Grundlagenforschung betreiben	do basic *research*
Produktreihen	product *ranges*
Medizintechnik	*medical* technology
Vorreiter auf einem Gebiet sein	be a torch-bearer in a *field*
viel von jemandem erwarten	*expect* a lot of someone
eine Herausforderung benötigen	need a *challenge*
mit einem Problem umgehen können	be able to *handle* a problem
eine Firma übernehmen	*take* a company *over*
Geschick im Umgang mit Menschen	*interpersonal* skills
ein Netz (persönlicher Beziehungen) aufbauen	*build* a network

TASK 2: Test your memory

1. He has been at MEDIQUIP for eight years. He has been doing basic research for all their ranges across the board.
2. He is ambitious and needs a challenge.
3. What interests Dr Kleinshirt most are Tissmann's interpersonal skills, the ability to handle the psychological problems that come with the culture clash.

TASK 3: Pitfalls for Germans

1. Learn about someone / get to know someone:
   I have to *get to know* the person in more detail.
   Of course, you could also say: *learn more about* a person.
2. take over / overtake – übernehmen / überholen
   Dr Kleinshirt should have said: 'And what about the situation that we are *taking over* their company?'

When driving in your car you can *overtake* cyclists if your car is fast enough.

3. meaning / opinion – Bedeutung / Meinung
   Dr Kleinshirt should have said: *'It's my opinion* that we have not to be too pushy.'
   A person may *have an opinion* or *be of the opinion* that ...
   A person's life or words may or may not *have a meaning* (Bedeutung, Sinn).
4. I'll just *remind* you of my activities until now.

TASK 4: Joke your way round trouble spots

brauchen =	benötigen (allgemein)	need
	Zeit, Energie etc. erfordern, um etwas zu erreichen	take (meist it *takes* ...)
	erfordern, weil etwas davon abhängt	require

1. How many psychiatrists does *it take* to change a light bulb?
   Only one. But the bulb must want to be changed.
2. It's the final proof of God's omnipotence that he doesn't *need* to exist in order to save us.
3. *It takes* a lot of experience for a girl to kiss like a beginner.
4. To err is human, but to really foul things up *requires* a computer.

TASK 5: Another trouble spot to joke around

remind someone of	jemanden erinnern an
remember	sich erinnern

1. Now that we've all enjoyed a wonderful meal, I'd like to *remind* you that wild, uninhibited applause burns up twenty-five calories a minute! So start burning! Cheers.
2. By the time you reach 75 years of age you've learnt everything. All you have to do is to try and *remember* it.

3. Only when the final draft of the document has been typed up and printed will the boss *remember* an important point that must be added to the middle of it.
4. I can't seem to *remember* you name, and please don't *remind* me!

TASK 6: Beef up your word power

1. If you'll *permit* me ...
2. And how do you *propose to do* that?
3. My first priority would be to *connect* with them mentally.
4. I have to get to know the person *in more detail.*

TASK 7: Spot the mistake

1. I'*ve been* at MEDIQUIP for eight years.
   Spricht man über einen Zeitraum, der bis zum Zeitpunkt des Sprechens andauert, nimmt man *present perfect.*
2. I *studied* medicine for my first degree.
3. And then I *did* a postgraduate qualification in marketing.
   Aufeinander folgende, abgeschlossene Situationen stehen im *simple past.*

TASK 8: Writing a CV

(1) *After* leaving school in 1976, I went to Italy for six months to study architecture. (2) *As soon* as I returned to England, I applied for a three-year architectural course. (3) *While* I was studying at Manchester University, I developed an interest in photography. (4) I left the university in April 1993 *before* taking/*before I took* my final exams in June and came to London. (5) I worked for an advertising agency *until* I had enough money to start a two-year diploma course in photography at Hamden College of Fine Arts which I completed in 1997. (6) *Since* qualifying/I qualified, I have been employed as a sports photographer by the Daily News. (7) However, *when* my contract finishes in March, I shall be available to start a new job immediately.

CHAPTER 3

TASK 1: Pitfalls for Germans

1. He was commissioned *by* the Board to go to MEDIMAKE in Nottingham.
   Merke: Passiv/Leideform – der Täter wird mit *by* angeschlossen.
2. *Among other things* he was to talk to key people to allay their fears.
3. Mrs Sparkler, *Tissmann speaking*. I need your help.
4. *I will be staying* there *for* at least three months.
   Nicht verzweifeln: 1. Wenn Sie über eine Situation in der Zukunft reden, die Teil Ihrer Planung ist, nehmen Sie *will + be + ing-form.*
   2. *for* three months: Zeiträume werden mit *for* benannt.

TASK 2: Build your phrases for flying the friendly skies

Ich möchte gerne einen Flug nach London buchen.	I'd *like to* book a flight to London.
Einfach oder hin und zurück?	Single or *return*?
Was kostet der Flug zur Zeit?	What's *the price of* the flight at the moment?
Erste Klasse oder Touristenklasse?	Do you want to fly first class or *economy*?
Und wie sieht es mit dem Rückflug aus?	And *what about* the return flight?
Wann, sagten Sie, startet die Maschine?	When does the plane *take* off, did you say?
Ist das Ortszeit?	Is that *local time*?
Ist es dort früher oder später als bei uns?	Are they *ahead* of us or behind us?
Ihr Anschlussflug ist um 14 Uhr.	Your *connecting* flight is at 2.00 p.m.
Sie haben zwei Stunden Aufenthalt in Chicago.	You'll have a *2-hour layover / stop-over* in Chicago.

TASK 3: More pitfalls for Germans

1. Dr Tissmann doesn't smoke.
2. Yes, it's all *up to date*. Could you confirm your booking by fax, please?

TASK 4: Build your phrases for a good night's rest

Ich möchte gern ein Zimmer reservieren.	I'd like to book a room, *please.*
Wie lange möchten Sie bleiben?	How long *would* you like to *stay*?
Auf welchen Namen, bitte?	*In what* name, please?
Einzel- oder Doppelzimmer?	*Single* or *double*?
Was kostet das für eine Nacht?	*How much* is that per night?
Ist das Frühstück inbegriffen?	Does that *include* breakfast?
Leider muss ich meine Reservierung stornieren.	I'm afraid I have to *cancel* my booking.
Würden Sie das bitte per Fax bestätigen?	Would you *confirm* that *by* fax, please?

TASK 5: Tricky words

A: The question of GM (genetically manipulated) food is of *topical* interest. What is the Government's *current* stand on biogenetics?

B: No need to worry, they say. *Actually*, scientists are not sure at all.

A: By the way, the list you gave me yesterday containing the test results of GM food is not *up-to-date.*

B: I know, those were the glossed-over results from the producers. The *actual* results are in the pipeline.

TASK 6: Spot the mistake

1. *I'm flying* to Manchester airport *next week.*
   Merke: Spricht man 1.) über Arrangements für die Zukunft und erwähnt 2.) eine Zeitangabe der Zukunft (*next week*), dann nimmt man die Verlaufsform der Gegenwart (*present progressive*).
2. *I'm phoning* from Germany.
   Merke: Spricht man davon, was man gerade tut, dann nimmt man die Verlaufsform der Gegenwart (*present progressive*).
3. And how long *will* you *be staying*?
   Merke: Wenn Sie über eine Situation in der Zukunft reden, die Teil Ihrer Planung ist, nehmen Sie *will + be + ing-form.*
4. I *saw* your hotel advertised in the Internet.
   Merke: Der Sprecher bezieht sich auf die Situation, als er am Computer saß. Er sieht diese Situation als abgeschlossen.

CHAPTER 4

TASK 1: Key words in business

ein Pass ist abgelaufen	a passport has *expired*
nicht mehr gültig sein	be no longer *valid*
einen Pass erneuern lassen	*have* one's passport *renewed*
So sind die Vorschriften hier.	These are the *rules* here.

TASK 2: Could you correct the mistakes in the text?

1. Good afternoon, sir, could I see your passport, please? – Certainly, *here you are.*
2. I'll be *attending* some conferences. (For more information see Tasks 4 and 5.)
3. I'm *a* member of the European Union, you know.
   Merke: Der unbestimmte Artikel *a/an* steht vor der Zugehörigkeit zu einer Gruppe: Beruf, Nationalität, Partei, Religion etc. (see also chapter 2).

TASK 3: Talk your way through the passport control

Passport control	You
What's your *nationality*?	I'm German.
What's the *purpose* of your visit?	I'm here *on business.*
I'm afraid your passport has *expired.*	Too bad! Can I *have* it *renewed at* my consulate?
How long *are* you *planning* to stay?	I'*ll be staying for* a week.
Have you got anything to *declare*?	No, I've only articles for my personal *use.*

TASK 4: Tricky words

(1) see (2) attending (3) goes to (4) pay a visit (5) visit (6) go and see

TASK 5: More tricky words

Another cup of tea?	*Yes, please.*
May I use your phone?	*Of course, go ahead.*
Have you got an aspirin for me?	*Here you are.*
Thank you for helping me.	*You're welcome.*

TASK 6: Could you correct the mistakes in the text?

1. *I've been waiting* for my luggage *for* more than half an hour.
   Merke: seit = *for* für Zeiträume (seit 14 Tagen)
   seit = *since* für Zeitpunkte (seit, ab letzter Woche)
   Present perfect, weil von einem Zeitraum die Rede ist, der bis zum Zeitpunkt des Sprechens noch andauert.

2. I only *noticed* the destination, Manchester.
   Merke: bemerken mit dem Mund: *remark*
   bemerken mit dem Auge: *notice*

Boss: I hope you don't mind me saying this, but there's a lot of dust on your desk! It looks as if it hasn't been cleaned *for* months.
Cleaning lady: Don't blame me, sir. I have only been here *since* last week.

"I'm not my usual self tonight," Tom *remarked.*
"Yes, I've *noticed* the improvement."

CHAPTER 5

TASK 1: Test your memory

1. An English friend had advised him not to rent a car at the airport because it would be cheaper in the nearest village.
2. He wants a comfortable car with a manual gear change. It shouldn't be too expensive.
3. Dave does not trust Tissmann's driving licence because it is old and only in German. He requires a European standard driving licence.

TASK 2: Keywords in business

ein Auto mieten	to *rent* a car
ein Auto mit Schaltautomatik	a car with automatic *transmission*
Sie wünschen Gangschaltung?	You want a *manual* gear change?
ein Budget einhalten müssen	have a budget to *keep* to
knapp bei Kasse sein	be *short* of money
Es hängt vom Preis ab.	It *depends* on the price.
unbeschränkte Kilometerzahl	unlimited *mileage*
Vollkaskoversicherung	fully *comprehensive* insurance
im Preis inbegriffen	*included* in the price
ein Verfahren einhalten müssen	have a *procedure* to go through
ein Formular ausfüllen	*fill out* a form
Wo ist Ihr ständiger Wohnsitz?	What's your *permanent* address?

TASK 3: Pitfalls for Germans

1. Word order: I wouldn't *exactly say* that.
2. What's your permanent address? – *13*, Kleinschmidtstrasse in 69115 Heidelberg.
3. May I have a look at your driving licence, please? – *Here you are.*
4. You're not going to *do* business with me?
5. Idiom: This place is *at the back of beyond*.

TASK 4: Beef up your word power

Can I be of assistance?	Can *I help you*?
I'd rather have a comfortable car.	I'd *prefer* a comfortable car.
I want to say I don't like automatic transmissions.	I *mean* I don't like automatic transmissions.

TASK 5: Joke your way round trouble spots

1. "Waiter! Waiter! What is this fly *doing* in my soup?" – "Hmm ... Looks like breast-stroke, doesn't it?"
2. "I've prepared the turkey," said Ronny to his girlfriend. "I've plucked it and stuffed it. All you've got to *do* is kill it and cook it."
3. A hedgehog finding himself on top of a scrubbing brush: "We all *make* mistakes, don't we?"

TASK 6: More about trouble maker: machen

eine Prüfung machen	*take* / *do* an exam
Urlaub machen	*go* on holiday
Überstunden machen	*do* overtime
eine Geschäftsreise machen	*go on* a business trip
jemanden verantwortlich machen	*hold* someone responsible

If more than one person can *be held responsible*,
nobody will be found to blame. (hold, held, held)

Last year we were on the edge of an abyss –
This year we've *taken* a big step forward.

TASK 7: Rent your car

1. I'm not used to automatic *transmission*.
2. I'd prefer a car with a *manual gear change*.
3. What does the insurance *cover*?
4. Is fully *comprehensive* insurance *included* in the price?
5. How much is the daily *rental* for a Ford Cortina?
6. Where can I *return* the car in Glasgow?

CHAPTER 6

TASK 1: Key words in business

ein Zimmer reservieren	*reserve* a room
ausgebucht sein	be *fully* booked
ein Hotel empfehlen	*recommend* a hotel
bei einer Firma arbeiten	work *at* a company
eine Reklamation haben	have a *complaint* to make
sich über den Service beschweren	*complain* about the service
einen Gast in einem anderen Zimmer unterbringen	*relocate* a guest to another room
Entschuldigen Sie die Unannehmlichkeiten.	Sorry for any *inconvenience* caused.

TASK 2: Pitfalls for Germans

1. The Victoria. Can you show it me on this *map*?
2. I'm *not used to driving* in such a big city as Nottingham.
3. I'm going to *check* the information in my fax from you.
4. After all, there's a lot of *competition* in your business and my company *may be using* your service very often.

Attention please!

concurrence = A. agreement, B. coincidence

A. The manager's proposals met with *concurrence* among the members of the board.

B. Two or more things happening at the same time: an unfortunate concurrence of events.

Konkurrenz = competition

The new computer products met with fierce *competition* from abroad.

TASK 3: Test your memory

1. He told him that he was travelling the wrong way up a one-way street.
2. There is no reservation for a Mr Tissmann, but for a Mr Mediquip.
3. The toilet didn't flush, the tap was dripping and the room was too noisy.

TASK 4: Beef up your word power

So that's *settled.*	So that's *solved.*
There is a *booking* for a Mr M.	There is a *reservation* for a Mr M.
We'll *move* you to another room.	We'll *relocate* you to another room.
If I *may interrupt* you, sir.	If I *could break in*, sir.

TASK 5: Joke your way round trouble spots

1. Without a *map* you'll lose your way
   on your trip to the Hudson Bay.
2. You buy a *ticket*
   to watch cricket.
3. Tom signs his *cards*
   with 'kind regards'.
4. A manager without his *briefcase*
   is in the office out of place.

TASK 6: More tricky words

kontrollieren =	überprüfen, nachprüfen	check
	überwachen, regeln	control

1. Tissmann's passport was *checked* by the immigration officer.
2. He was going to *check* the information in the fax from the hotel.
3. A policeman was *controlling* the traffic at the traffic island.
4. Why is it that this company cannot *control* its cashflow?

eventuell	possible, possibly, perhaps, may be
schließlich, endlich	eventual(ly), finally, at last

1. He *eventually* reached the airport.
2. He had a street map in order to avoid *possible* traffic jams.
3. My company will *perhaps* use your service very often.

TASK 7: Let's test your memory

1. I've a *reservation in the name of* Meier.
2. Is there any *message for* me?
3. Do you want *full board* or only *bed and breakfast*?
4. I'd like to *see* the manager. I've got a *complaint* to make.
5. Could you *get my bill ready*?
6. Could I have a *separate bill* for the calls?

TASK 8: A mixed bag of questions

1. What do you put into the hotel safe?	your *valuables*
2. Another word for booking:	*reservation*
3. The document you have to fill in?	*registration form*
4. Three meals at the hotel:	*full board*
5. They clean and iron your clothes:	*laundry service*
6. If you are not satisfied, you make a	*complaint*
7. You want a detailed bill. Ask for an	*itemised* bill

CHAPTER 7

TASK 1: Key words in business

Wir haben bis 20 Uhr geöffnet.	We *are* open till 8pm.
Wir schließen um 19 Uhr.	We *close* at 7pm.
Welche Größe haben Sie?	*What's* your *size*?
Fühlen Sie einmal das Material.	*Feel* the material!
Ich führe diese Waren nicht.	I don't *stock* these goods.
Wir verkaufen nur gegen bar.	I'm a *cash only* shop.
Das ist ein Schnäppchen.	It's a *real bargain.*
Geld aus dem Automaten holen	get money from a *cash dispenser*
keine Nachfrage nach Mangos	no *call for* mangos

TASK 2: Pitfalls for Germans

1. I'm *sweating like hell.*
2. I *have my suitcase* packed by my secretary.
3. I want a ... *novel.*
4. A novel with a background in *technology.*
5. *Have you got any* pineapples?
6. There's a *cash dispenser near* my hotel.
   Aber: There's a cash dispenser *nearby.*

TASK 3: Test your memory

1. He should ask for an eight and a half.
2. In Rome, of course. There you can buy novels and talk to Romans of both sexes.
3. You weigh things in pounds and you pay for them in pounds.

TASK 4: Beef up your word power

What can I do for you?	How *can I help you*?
What size do you take?	What'*s your size*?
I'm talking about a book.	I'm *referring to* a book.

You've never seen anything like those before.	You've never seen the *likes of them* before.
I'll take a kilo.	I'll *have* a kilo.
Do you accept cards?	Can I *pay with* a card?

TASK 5: Joke your way around trouble spots

schließen	schließen	close, shut
	abschließen	lock

1. Modern architecture: "In my experience, if you have to keep the lavatory door *shut (closed)* by extending your left leg, it's modern architecture.
2. Etiquette is knowing how to yawn with your mouth *closed (shut).*
3. Two business partners went fishing one Sunday together. As they were waiting for a nibble one suddenly exclaimed, "I think I forgot to *lock* the office safe!".
   "Don't worry," said his partner, "after all, we're both here."
4. I went down the street to the 24-hour grocery. When I got there, the guy was *locking* the front door. I said, "Hey, why are you *closing*? The sign says you're open 24 hours." He said, "Yes, but not in a row."

TASK 6: More trouble spots to joke around

lassen	leave	lassen, wo und wie es ist; überlassen
	let do	tun lassen, zulassen, erlauben
	let in, out	herein-, hinauslassen
	get, have done	etwas machen lassen; erledigen lassen

1. Father: Nonsense, *let* him walk to school like I did.
2. "You can't *have* your hair cut in office time."
   "So I didn't *get / have* it all cut off," he replied.
3. Boy: I can't read. I can't write, and the teacher won't even *let* me talk.
4. Just *leave* the most difficult problems for the laziest managers to solve.

CHAPTER 8

TASK 1: Key words in business

Kontakte mit Leuten in Schlüsselpositionen anbahnen	make *contacts* with *key* people
übers Geschäft reden	talk *business*
Angelegenheiten besprechen	discuss *matters*
Die Firma wurde 1970 gegründet.	The firm was *founded* in 1970.
die Produktpalette erneuern	*innovate* the product *range*
in den europäischen Markt eindringen	*break into* the European market
Strategien und Ziele *verfolgen*	*follow* strategies and *objectives*
die Kontrollmehrheit übernehmen	take a *controlling* interest
auf demselben Gebiet tätig sein	be in the same *field*

TASK 2: Pitfalls for Germans

A. Cultural mistakes

1. "Just call me John," Mr Gaylor said. He wanted to be on first name terms with Tissmann.
The correct response should have been: "Glad to meet you, John. I'm Uwe."

2. His first words should have been: "Uwe Tissmann speaking."

B. Idiomatic mistakes

3. I (had) thought we would *talk business.*

4. I'll *have* a fruit juice.

5. Could I *speak* to John Gaylor, please? Is he *in*?

C. False friends

6. Oh, *it's all the same to me*. When do you have time?

7. I think the European market can be quite *profitable.*
rentable: zu mieten

D. Grammar

8. Fine. I'm looking forward to *seeing* you.
Nach Präpositionen folgt die -ing Form des Verbs,
aber: I'm looking forward to *our meeting*.

TASK 3: Test your memory

Do you remember how they ...?

offered assistance	How *can I help* you? What *can I do for* you?
asked for a caller's name	Who *shall I say is calling*, sir?
said they didn't understand	I didn't *catch* it first time.
connected a caller	*Putting* you *through*.
suggested a meeting time	*Let's make it* this afternoon, shall we?
suggested a meeting point	*What about going* to a pub?

TASK 4: Joke your way round trouble spots

1. Judge: What *did* your husband *say* when you smashed up the new car?
   Wife: He *didn't say* a word.
2. A diplomat is a man who can *tell you to* go to hell in such a way that you actually look forward to the trip.
3. "You look worried. What *did* the doctor *say*?"
   "He *told me to* take these pills for the rest of my life."
4. How can I *tell* that you are *speaking / telling* the truth?
   It takes two to *speak / tell* the truth – one to *speak* and one to hear.
5. Today I dialled a wrong number. The other person *said*, "Hello" and I *said*, "Hello, could I *speak* to Joey?" He *said*, "Ugh... I don't think so ... he's only two months old." I *said*, "*Tell* him that I'll wait."

These are the rules:

1. **A.** *say* wird benutzt, wenn keine Ergänzung folgt:
   That's exactly what I said.
   B. *say + (that)*: in der indirekten Rede:
   She said that she was going home.
2. **A.** *tell:* verlangt eine Ergänzung (Objekt), entweder eine Person oder etwas Abstraktes:
   She never tells the truth.
   I told her that I wasn't coming to the wedding.
   B. *tell someone to do something* ist eine Aufforderung:
   I told him not to smoke in bed.

TASK 5: Typical mistakes on the phone

1. Who would you like to speak to?
2. Could I ask who *I'm speaking* to?
3. I'm sorry, sir. I *didn't quite catch* your name.
4. *Am I speaking* to ROBOTALOT in Bonn?

TASK 6: Making an appointment

1. I was wondering if we could possibly *meet* next week.
2. What day would *suit* you best?
3. *Shall* we *say* Tuesday?
4. Would you like us to arrange *accommodation* for you?

TASK 7: Arranging place and time

1. I'm *calling* to check the time of Monday's meeting.
2. How long *do* you *think* we'll need?
3. So, we'*re meeting* at my hotel on the 12th of March.
4. I look forward to *seeing* you on the 12th.

CHAPTER 9

TASK 1: Key words in business

Dürfte ich um Ihre Aufmerksamkeit bitten?	Could I *have your attention*, please?
Sie haben das Wort.	The *floor* is yours.
Missverständnisse aufklären	*clear up* misunderstandings
jemandes Hoffnungen übertreffen	*exceed* someone's expectations
vor einer Firmenfusion stehen	be *involved* in a merger
Brücken zu seinen Partnern bauen	*build bridges* to one's partners
eine Aufgabe erledigen	*achieve* a task
prüfen, welche Umsätze erzielt werden	*check* what *turnovers* are made

TASK 2: Pitfalls for Germans

1. Colleagues, I want to be *brief.*
   I want to be *short* ist das Gegenteil von I want to be *tall* (*Körpergröße*).
2. *In most cases* we all have nothing to fear.
3. But this *needn't* mean *dismissals* (*to fire* see Task 5).
4. My present level leaves a lot *to be desired.*

TASK 3: Test your memory

1. What rumours or misunderstandings does Tissmann have to clear up?
   There will be no takeover or dismissals.
2. How does he describe his mission at MEDIMAKE?
   He is on a reconnaissance (check products, markets, turnovers) and is creating common ground (build bridges).
3. What is the task lying ahead of both companies?
   To prepare a merger, identify parallel work and complicated processes.

TASK 4: Beef up your word power

✔ fusion

1. joint venture	3. fusion
2. merger	4. takeover

TASK 5: Joke your way round trouble spot 'must'

must not	nicht tun dürfen
not to have to	nicht tun müssen
need not	nicht zu tun brauchen

1. Two salesman met again after a night of hard drinking. "We *mustn't* drink that much again," said Jones to Smith. "Do you remember that last night you sold Tower Bridge?"
   "Is that all?" – "No, I bought it."
2. It's the final proof of God's omnipotence that he *need not* exist in order to save us. PETER DE VRIES
3. An Italian prime minister *must not* think of getting married until he gets a steady job.
4. Looking out of their tent, James and John saw a lion. The lion was coming nearer. James put his trainers on. "Why are you doing that?" John asked, "You are not faster than the lion!" – "I *don't have to* be faster than the lion," replied James, "I only *mustn't* be slower than you!"
5. A German business man entered a Swiss bank. He looked carefully around, went to the reception desk and whispered, "I want to invest 300,000 marks." – "You *needn't* whisper," said the bank clerk, "poverty is nothing to be ashamed of."

TASK 6: Have a joke with 'most'

der, die, das meiste	*höchster Grad*: mehr als alle anderen, mehr als je zuvor	the most
am meisten	*hoher Grad*: fast alle(s), der größte Teil, die Mehrheit	most

1. When I was young I thought money was *the most* important thing in life. Now that I am old I know that it is. OSCAR WILDE
2. *Most* women are not as young as they are painted.
3. Doctor: Say 'aaaaaah.'
   Girl: That's a change! *Most* young men want me to say 'yes'.

4. Selling is *the most* exciting thing you can do with your clothes on. JOHN FENTON
5. One girl told her friend, "He not only lied to me about his yacht, but I had to do *most* of the rowing."
6. A breakfast meeting is *the most* uncivilised idea I've ever heard of. If you're going to have a breakfast meeting, it should be in bed with a beautiful woman. GORDON WHITE
7. Suicide is *the most* sincere form of self-criticism.
8. Ronald: Doctor, doctor my hands are trembling all the time.
   Doctor: I think you have got an alcohol problem.
   Ronald: Yes, doctor, I spill *most* of it.
9. Just leave *the most* difficult problems for the laziest managers to solve. They will come up with the quickest solutions.
10. People who can least afford to pay rent, pay rent. People who can *most* afford to pay rent, build up equity. MURPHY'S LAW

TASK 7: Odd phrase out

I'm glad	that you're sacrificing one hour of your valuable time to listen to me.

I'm glad ist Ausdruck der Freude, nicht des Dankes wie *I appreciate* und *I'm grateful.*

TASK 8: Let's woggle a few speechfunctions

1. Ladies and Gentlemen, could I have your *attention* for a moment?
2. I'm not going to *waste* your valuable time. I want to be *brief.*
3. I'm grateful for having been offered the opportunity to *clear* up some *misunderstandings.*

TASK 9: More tricky words

1. I *rise (sich erheben)* to toast the prosperity of our companies.
2. Let's *raise (etwas erheben)* our glasses to the future of MEDIMAKE and MEDIQUIP.
3. Advice to speakers: *Stand up (sich erheben)*, speak up, shut up.

CHAPTER 10

TASK 1: Key words in business

Wie sind die Öffnungszeiten?	What are the *opening hours / office hours*?
Wie viel Ausstellungsfläche haben Sie angemietet?	How much *exhibition space* have you *rented*?
Der Termin war zu knapp.	The *deadline* was too *short.*
Es ist nur ein Ausstellungsstück.	It's only *on display.*
Es hat die Größe einer Armbanduhr.	It is the *size* of a wristwatch.
seine Waren vorführen	present one's *wares*
Die Preisangaben sind falsch.	Prices are *wrongly quoted.*
Die Fotos sind unscharf.	The photos are *out of focus.*
einige Werte eingeben	*enter* some *parameters*
ein unverkäufliches Muster	a *sample* that is not for *sale*

TASK 2: Pitfalls for Germans

1. *You don't say!* (Idiom)
2. I can *imagine*. (*imagine* ist nicht reflexiv, kein Pronomen)
3. Couldn't you do *anything* about it? (meist in Frage- und verneinten Sätzen; siehe Task 4).
4. I'm interested in your *latest* product. (das letzte = neueste)
5. Have you got a *prospectus* for the range? (see note and Task 5)

Attention please!

prospects (Plural): The chances of being successful.
Further training would improve your *job prospects.* Long-term *employment prospects* for young people still look gloomy.
prospect: a potential customer or a candidate or competitor who is likely to be successful. She's a good *prospect* for the American team.

TASK 3: Beef up your word power

1. Macrosoft presents its *wares* at the major trade fairs.
2. It says on the bottle '*Produce* of France'.
3. We are marketing a range of beauty *products*.
4. Should I collect the *goods*, or do you deliver them?
5. The poor devil peddles his handmade *wares* in a street market.

articles made of silver or a metal that look like silver knives, forks, dishes, etc used at meals:	*silverware*
dishes that can be used for cooking food in an oven:	*ovenware*
household equipment and tools, pans, nails and brushes:	*hardware*
pots, dishes, etc made of baked clay:	*earthenware*

TASK 4: Joke your way round trouble spots

1. An intellectual is a man who has found *something* more interesting than women.
2. Never invest your money in *anything* that eats or needs repairing.
3. Specialists are people who know everything about nothing and nothing about *anything* else.
4. A holiday is *something* you have for two weeks that takes fifty weeks to pay for.
5. "What's all this fuss about plutonium?" said Annette. "How can *something* named after a Disney character be dangerous?"
6. An expert is a man who is like a eunuch in a harem – he knows all about it but can't do *anything* about it.
7. The longer one saves *something* before throwing it away, the sooner it will be needed after it is thrown away.
8. "Well, I found out early in life that you didn't have to explain *something* you didn't say."

TASK 5: More trouble spots to joke around

1. "But your *brochure / prospectus* says £10."
2. The *latest* kind of computer was presented at the Cebit in Hannover.
3. Can you *imagine* an entire city under glass? (nichtreflexives Verb)
4. A caller who dials the wrong number will call a second time as soon as you have returned to your living room and *made yourself comfortable* (reflexives Verb).

Attention please!

newest: not existing before; introduced, made, invented, recently or for the first time

latest: the fashion / trend; her latest novel; the latest developments / discoveries. Have you heard the latest news?

last: coming after all others in time or order.
What time does the last bus leave? The last novel she wrote before she died.

TASK 6: Let's go woggling again

1. We'd like to take *part* in the exhibition.
2. How long does the fair last?
3. We wish to apply for *exhibition* space.
4. Can you *quote* us the price per square metre?

TASK 7: Beef up your word power again

stand	*booth*
booking	*reservation*
take part in a fair	*participate* in a fair
free tickets	*complimentary* tickets

TASK 8: Printed matter

1	catalogue of	D	exhibitors
2	sales	B	literature
3	promotional	A	material
4	list of	C	visitors

CHAPTER 11

TASK 1: Key words in business

einen Vergleichstest machen	do a *benchmarking* (test)
sich um einen Auftrag über zehn Rollstühle bewerben	*tender* for ten wheelchairs
Preisangebote erhalten	receive *quotations*
Wir stellen besondere Anforderungen.	We have special *requirements.*
Wir haben die technischen Angaben überprüft.	We've *checked* specifications.
Das ist genau das, was wir brauchen.	That *exactly fits* the bill.
ein maßgeschneidertes Produkt	a *customised* product
typische Produkteigenschaften	typical *product features*
viele Neuerungen aufweisen	*feature* many innovations
Der Verschleiß ist vernachlässigbar.	The *wear and tear* is negligible.
Diese Teile sind im zentralen Ersatzteillager erhältlich.	These parts are *available* in the Spare Parts Centre.

TASK 2: Pitfalls for Germans

1. It's our company philosophy to present our brochures to serious *entrepreneurs* like yourself as clearly as possible.
   undertakers: Leichenbestatter – Unternehmer: *entrepreneur*
2. Our company is much *bigger* now. (See Task 6)
3. Our earlier ranges had some *serious* problems. (See Task 5)
4. These parts are immediately available at any *sports department store.*
   department store: Warenhaus, Kaufhaus; warehouse: Lager
5. Well, that *is a thing of the past* (idiom).

TASK 3: Test your memory

1. Why did Tissmann accompany Nathan Dealer?
   Tissmann wanted to do a benchmarking, that is to take similar products, one produced in Germany, one in GB and compare how they are sold.
2. Do you remember the features of the Bronco?
   The chair has specially *designed* super thin rims, it is *constructed* of aluminium, is *light* and *stable* and has recently *passed* the turtle test.

TASK 4: Beef up your word power

1. Four companies have made a tender for the construction work.
   We will accept the lowest *tender.*
2. I'm waiting for the latest *quotations* from the Stock Exchange.
3. I've had an *offer* of £2,200 for the old Rolls Royce. This is an *offer* that I can't refuse.
4. Advert in the press: Lady's bike £35 *ono.*

TASK 5: Joke your way round trouble spots

ernst	earnest(ly)	Gegenteil von: heiter
	serious(ly)	seriös, ernst zu nehmen

1. The *serious* music lover is the bloke who, hearing a soprano in the bathroom, puts his ear to the keyhole.
2. "In your references it says your are an extremely *earnest* fellow, without imagination and a 'yes-man' with no sense of humour at all. In most professions all these things would be a *serious* drawback. In accountancy they are a positive asset."
3. I have come to the conclusion that politics is too *serious* a matter to be left to the politicians. CHARLES DE GAULLE
4. The best way to tell if a man is honest is to *earnestly* ask him if he is honest. If he says he is, you know he's a crook.

TASK 6: More trouble spots to joke through

1. Napoleon may not have been a *tall* man, but for many he was a *great* statesman.
2. My aunt hid a *large* sum of money and jewellery before she died. My lawyer has arranged a seance with a medium to inquire about its whereabouts.
3. Adolescence: the period in which the young suddenly feel a *great* responsibility to answer the telephone.
4. If you are a *big* enough company, your mistakes become standards. Just take the example of Microsoft.

Attention, please!

You can use *big* or *large* to describe animals, objects, places, etc. *Big* is more common in spoken language: *They live in a big / large house.*
Large is used for sizes of things you buy: *small, medium or large.*
A large number / amount / quantity of something can also be a more formal way of saying *'a lot of': They spent a large amount of money on their daughter's wedding.*
You use *great* to describe somebody or something that is important or has an impressive quality: *a great artist, the great Pacific Ocean. Peter the Great was a Russian ruler.*
Great can be used with uncountable nouns: *It gives me great pleasure to announce the winner.*
Tall refers to the height of people or things: *Tom is over six feet tall.*

TASK 7: Complete the dialogue

Customer	Salesman
Pleased to meet you.	The *pleasure* is mine.
I'm afraid I can't spare you more than an hour.	Well, let's *come straight* to the point. / *I'll be brief.*
What we need are customised wheelchairs.	I assure you that we can *meet* your *needs* exactly.
What about your competitors?	Our wheelchair has *passed* all the *benchmarking* tests.

CHAPTER 12

TASK 1: Key words in business

große Probleme bekommen	*run into* serious problems
Waagen rationell montieren	*erect* scales efficiently
potentielle Kunden anregen	*stimulate* our *potential* customers
Händlern Rabatte anbieten	offer *discounts* to *dealers*
Die Produktreihe besteht aus vier Elementen.	The product range *consists* of four pieces.
Die Gewinnspanne ist minimal.	The profit *margin* is minimal.

TASK 2: Pitfalls for Germans

1. *What (what sort / kind of)* problems? (see also Task 4)
   What vor Substantiv fragt nach den Eigenschaften von Personen und Sachen:
   Was für Bücher? — What books?
   Was für Leute? — What people?
   Aber: *What* vor Verben verlangt die Präposition in Endstellung:
   Für was brauchst du es? — What do you need it for?
   Für was interessierst du dich? — What are you interested in?
2. Last week I *visited* the *factory*.
   Past tense wegen *last week*. *Fabric* ist das Gewebe, die Stoffart: *woollen / silk / cotton fabrics; a striped fabric.*
3. Sex life? How *vulgar / primitive*!
   Aber: I'm just an *ordinary* man: Ich bin ein ganz gewöhnlicher Mann.
4. I'm sure I don't wish *every* Tom, Dick and Harry to know my body data.
   jeder (unbestimmte Anzahl): *every*
   jeder (aus einer bestimmten Anzahl): *each* ... (see also Task 6)
5. And don't forget the generous *commission* that the dealers get.
   Another pair of false friends:
   Provision: *commission*, *provision*: Versorgung
6. And my suggestion would be to go back to the customers and *enquire* about what they really need.
   We ordinary people *enquire,* the police *inquires* or *investigates.*

TASK 3: Test your memory

1. The problems discussed at the meeting:
   ☑ low profit margins ☑ high discounts for dealers
   ☑ no customer orientation ☑ weak demand
2. It's a misunderstanding:
   a) Tissmann confuses *ordinary* and 'ordinär'.
   b) He missed the pause after the comma between *'sex, life expectancy'*.

TASK 4: Joke your way round trouble spots

Was für ein(e) ... !	What a ... !	für zählbare Dinge
	What ... !	für nichtzählbare (messbare) Dinge
Ausnahmen:	What a pity! Wie schade! What a shame! Was für eine Schande!	

1. *What a* salesman!
2. *What a* turnover!
3. But look *what state* it is in.
4. *What a* wonderful way to die!
5. *What size* is your alligator?

TASK 5: More trouble spots to joke around

jede / r/ s	each:	jeder Einzelne (aus einer bestimmten Anzahl)
	every:	jeder, alle (unbestimmte Anzahl)

1. Boss: "It hasn't escaped me that *every time* Liverpool is playing at home mid-week you ask permission to go and visit your grandmother who's seriously ill."
2. "We've marked them down to a pound *each* but they still won't sell."
   Price them at two pounds *each*.
   Send six out to *each* of our best clients.
   Every customer returned the parcel ...
3. He ordered two chinchillas for his wife. One for *each* chin.

TASK 6: Let's woggle around meetings

1. Ladies and Gentlemen, I *declare* the meeting open.
2. Would anybody wish to *add* an item / point to the agenda?
3. Who is going to *keep* the minutes today?
4. There are three decisions to be *taken* today.
5. Is there any other *business*?
6. Let's *put* it to the vote.
7. The motion is *carried* by seven votes to four.

CHAPTER 13

TASK 1: Key words in business

ein Gerät	a piece of *equipment*
auf den Markt bringen	*launch* on the market
nagelneu auf dem Markt	*brand new* on the market
Kontakte zu Partnern herstellen	*make* connections to partners
Welches sind die Vorzüge?	*What* are the *benefits*?

TASK 2: Phrases for presenters

eine Präsentation machen	*make* a presentation
Das Thema dieser Präsentation ist ...	The *topic* of this presentation is ...
einen Überblick über das Produkt geben	give an *overview* of the product
ein Foto zeigen	*show* a photograph
Zeit für Fragen haben	*have* question *time*

TASK 3: Pitfalls for Germans

Tricky words and phrases

1. Then I'll *explain* its features and advantages.
   explain something to someone: erklären im Sinne von erläutern
   declare: erklären im Sinne von öffentlich erklären; mit Nachdruck sagen
2. *What does it look like? What ... like?* fragt nach der Beschaffenheit, dem Aussehen (siehe auch Task 6).
3. The Body & Soul Styler is very *humane* and also has proposals as to how the stressed manager can make connections to partners.
   human: menschlich im Gegensatz zu tierisch, pflanzlich, unbelebt
   humane: menschlich im Sinne von menschenfreundlich, gütig
4. The reason for his superman-like appearance is our company's *policies* to design and manufacture instruments ...
   politic: politisch

politics: party politics, government politics – Politik im Sinne von Wissenschaft oder Programm

policies: im Sinne von Strategie, Vorgehensweise

5. Forgive me if I *make / commit* any mistakes. (See also chapter 5, Task 5 and Task 6)

Tricky Grammar

6. First of all *I'll try* to give you an overview of this very innovative product. Versprechen und Voraussagen werden im *will-future* abgegeben.
7. This can include a few useful *pieces of advice* such as "go to the swimming pool in the next ten minutes."
   Advice ist nicht zählbar: *good advice; some advice*. Will man zählen, muss man wie im Deutschen ein 'zählbares Wort' hinzufügen:
   drei gute Rat*schläge:* three good / a few *pieces of* advice.

TASK 4: Test your memory

	True	False
1. The new product is best suited for fitness centres.		✔
2. The device is worn round the chest.		✔
3. It prevents you from getting overweight.	✔	
4. It has social functions, too.	✔	

TASK 5: Joke your way round trouble spots

wie	how	Frage nach Mittel, Art und Weise
	what	Frage nach Namen, Mengen-, Ortsangaben, Beschaffenheit
	as	Vergleiche: as ... as; same as; such as = wie zum Beispiel

1. A true gentleman is someone who knows *how* to play the trumpet but doesn't.
2. The director had never been so upset as when Margaret asked *what* he wanted to name the baby – Margaret, that's his secretary.
3. Money isn't everything. There are other things, such *as* jewellery, stocks and travellers cheques.

4. Funny *how* a wife can spot a blonde hair on a chap's coat, yet miss the garage doors.
5. When Noah sailed the waters blue,
   he had his troubles same *as* you.
   For forty days he drove the Ark
   before he found a place to park.

TASK 6: More trouble spots to joke around

1. "There, there," she consoled him. "Who says it was your *fault*?"
2. All great discoveries are made by *mistake*.
3. Nature always sides with the hidden *flaw*.
   Unfortunately, the hidden *flaw* never remains hidden.
4. The only real *errors* are human *errors*.
5. A doctor can bury his *mistakes*. An architect can only advise his client to plant vines.
6. A *defect* will not occur till a machine has passed final inspection.
7. Any *error* in any calculation will be in the direction of most harm.
8. No one is listening until you make a *mistake*.

Mistake: das häufigste Wort für Fehler, die man macht:
The letter had quite a few mistakes in it.
Going on a camping holiday with children was a mistake.

Error: für Fehler, Irrtum in Berechnungen – vor allem im technischen Bereich: *errors in calculations; a human error*: menschliches Versagen.

Fault: a) betont jemandes Verantwortung oder Schuld für den Fehler:
It was my fault.
b) Unvollkommenheit von Personen und Dingen:
There was a design fault in the train doors.
I accepted my father's faults because I loved him.

Flaw: für leichte, oft versteckte Mängel, die das Gesamtbild beeinträchtigen.
The vase is perfect except for a few small flaws in its base.
An argument full of flaws; a flaw in a contract.

TASK 7: Visual aids for presentations

slide	*transparency / OHP sheet*
handout	*chart, diagram*
screen	*graphics*

TASK 8: Word builder's corner

What's the *explanation* for this?	How can we *explain* this?
What are the *benefits* from this situation?	How can we *benefit* from this situation?
What are the *implications*?	What does this *imply*?

TASK 9: Tense and aspect

1. Mr X *will* now *speak* to you about ...
2. I *have been* a consultant to IBM for three years. (He still is a consultant to IBM.)
   I *was* ... (He no longer is a consultant to IBM.)
3. I*'ll try* to give you an overview of our activities.
4. In the handout I*'ll be passing* round, you*'ll find* ...

CHAPTER 14

TASK 1: Key words in business

einen Termin haben bei ...	have an *appointment* with ...
an einer Zusammenarbeit mit ... interessiert sein	be interested *in co-operation* with ...
neue Funktionen entwickeln	*develop* new features
das Fahrzeug beschreiben	describe the *vehicle*
Die Vorschriften der Regierung sind streng.	The rules *set by* the government are strict.
große Wachstumschancen	*large potential growth*

TASK 2: Pitfalls for Germans

Grammar

1. The wheelchair user is able to climb *safely* onto the pavement.
   safe ist Adjektiv; *safely* ist Adverb
2. Sorry, *if I'm boring* you with my ...? (See Task 6)
3. I'*m staying* here at this hotel. (See Task 6)
4. I *visited* the Persian Gulf last year.
   Last year ist Signal für in der Vergangenheit abgeschlossene Situationen, deshalb *past tense*. Wie der Name sagt, ist present perfect (*have visited*) keine Zeit der Vergangenheit.

Vocabulary

5. We don't *get* anything like that in Germany. (See Task 5A)
6. Yes, we have *the same / a similar* situation in Japan. (See Task 5B)
7. It's *difficult* to refuse this whisky. (See Task 5)

TASK 3: Cross-cultural mistakes

1. Well ... are you asleep, Mr Kowakawi?
   Geschlossene Augen sind in Japan ein Ausdruck der Konzentration.
2. I visited the Persian Gulf last year.
   Für Araber ist es ihr Golf (the Arabian Gulf) und gehört nicht zu Persien / Iran.
3. Please be my guest. Do try this whisky!
   Tissmann hätte wissen sollen, das Muslimen Alkohol verboten ist.

TASK 4: Joke your way round trouble spots

1. The young man asked the beautiful girl to marry him. He mentioned that that his father was 98 and very rich.
   She *became* his step-mother.
2. "You can't resign," said the circus manager to the human cannonball. "Where would I *get* another man of your calibre?"
3. Do not complain about *growing / getting* old.
   Many are denied the privilege.
4. "Doctor, I think I am *going* mad. Every time I ask someone the time I *get* a different answer.
5. A Scottish Wedding:
   Guest: "I believe she is your third daughter to *get* married, isn't she?"
   Jock: "Yes, and the confetti is *getting* dirtier each time."

Here a few rules for better understanding.

Become, get mit folgendem Adjektiv für Zustandswechsel.

Become ist gehobener, *get* wird mehr in der Umgangssprache verwendet.

Go (und *turn*) mit folgendem Adjektiv für unerwünschten Zustandswechsel:
He's going bald / deaf. The meat went bad. The milk turned sour.
Go (und *turn*) werden oft mit Farben verwendet:
Her fingers went blue with cold. Wait till the lights turn green.

Turn auch für Wetterwechsel: *It suddenly turned very cold.*

TASK 5: More trouble spots to joke around

A: Schwer

1. Hmmmm! I find this very *hard* to believe.
2. There are two things that are more *difficult* than making an after-dinner speech ...
3. In the museum visitors' book, under the heading "Reason for visit", someone had written: "*Heavy* shower."
4. It's *difficult* to get a man to understand something when his salary depends upon his not understanding it.

These notes might help you.

heavy: a) schwer für großes Gewicht: a *heavy* suitccase
b) schwer im übertragenen Sinn: a *heavy* meal; a *heavy* cold

difficult: schwierig, kompliziert: a *difficult* question.

hard: a) schwierig, schwer zu vollziehen: it's *hard* to decide; *hard* to say; in der Bedeutung "schwierig" sind *difficult* und *hard* oft austauschbar; *hard* ist umgangssprachlicher.
b) anstrengend: a *hard* job

B. Gleich

1. Teenagers express a burning desire to be different from anyone else, then dress exactly *alike.*
   alike: gleich, ähnlich im Aussehen
2. In our company all colleagues are *equal* – only the salaries aren't.
   equal: gleich an Rechten, gleich vor dem Gesetz
3. That essay on the dog is exactly word for word the *same* as your brother's."
   "Of course sir, it's the *same* dog."
   same: derselbe

TASK 6: Joking your way through grammar

1. The people who live above me.
2. I'm living beyond my income.
3. The director was leaving ...
   Where do you live?
4. An Indian was observing ... the people were enjoying.

CHAPTER 15

TASK 1: Key words in business

über die Sachlage informiert werden	*receive* a brief
einen Termin vereinbaren	*fix* an appointment
ein Einkaufsvolumen von 6 Millionen Pfund	a *purchasing volume* of £6 million
Was ist Ihre Einstellung zum Thema Eigenproduktion oder Zukauf?	What's your approach *on make* or buy?
Das ist ein heißes Eisen.	That's a *hot potato.*
alles außerhalb montieren lassen	get everything *assembled* outside
Sechs Produktreihen sind auf drei Teams verteilt.	Six product lines are *shared out* amongst three teams.
der Innendienst für die Verkäufer im Außendienst	the sales support for the *field sales* staff.
Schadenersatz zahlen müssen	have to pay *compensation/damages*

TASK 2: Pitfalls for Germans

1. It was very difficult to fix an *appointment* with you.
   appointment: Termin beim Arzt, beim Friseur, zum Vorstellungsgespräch
   date: private Verabredung, Rendezvous; Datum
   deadline: Fristablauf; letzter Termin, um etwas zu erledigen
2. They *deserve* a *prize* for the work they do.
   deserve: Anerkennungen verdienen
   earn: Geld verdienen
   price: der Preis, den man bezahlt
   prize: der Preis, der einem verliehen wird
3. It doesn't *save* money at all.
   save: Geld sparen; Leben retten
   spare: übrig haben: Can you spare me a minute?
   ersparen: spare someone the trouble of doing something
4. We're talking *at cross purposes.* (feststehender idiomatischer Ausdruck)

5. I suppose you get a lot of *damage* with components like these.
   damage: Schaden (*some damage*: einige Schäden, *a lot of damage*: viele Schäden).
   damages: Schadenersatz (*claim damages*: Schadenersatz fordern)
6. I *was* out helping to sell with one of them two weeks ago.
   Past tense wird verwendet für in der Vergangenheit abgeschlossene Situationen, das Signal dafür ist: *two weeks ago.*

TASK 3: Test your memory

	True	False
1. First, they visited the assembly hall and workshops.		✔
2. The purchasing department is on the sixth floor.		✔
3. About fifteen people sell goods for £6 million.		✔
4. They don't outsource any more.		✔
5. Six product lines are shared out amongst 25 employees.	✔	

TASK 4: Joke your way round trouble spots

verdienen – is it *earn* or *deserve*?

1. Democracy is a system that ensures that we shall be governed no better than we *deserve*. G.B. SHAW
2. How much do you *earn*?

Preis – is it *price* or *prize*?

1. It's terrible bringing up a family today, considering the *price* of beer and cigarettes.
2. Steve Helms has been awarded the first *prize* for the best salesman of the year.
3. How do you double the *price* of a Trabbi?

Let's double check it

"I really don't *deserve* this *prize*. But then, I've got arthritis and I didn't *deserve* that either."

Verabredung, Termin –
is it *date, deadline* or *appointment*?

1. I had an *appointment* with my doctor this morning.
2. A. This product will help you get *dates* with bikini models.
   B. This product will save you time and money, which you'll need if you want to *date* bikini models.
   C. If you buy this product, you'll look like a bikini model.
3. Can we fix a *date* for the next meeting?
4. I'd better get a move on – next week is the *deadline* for handing in my application.

Is it *damage* or *damages*?

1. The storm had caused some *damage*.
2. He sued the company and won £5,000 (in) *damages*.
3. If there is a possibility of several things going wrong, the one that will cause the most *damage* will be the one to go wrong.

TASK 5: More trouble spots to joke around

1. We have to *wear* our helmets in the assembly plant.
2. "Do you sell pillow cases?"
   "Yes, Sir. What size do you need?"
   "I really don't know, but I *wear* a size seven hat."
3. Our modern world is so full of problems that if Moses came down from Mount Sinai again, the two tablets he'd be *carrying* would be aspirins.
4. I put the wrong size of battery in the beeper that I *wear* on my belt. The first call I got blew my shoes off.
5. Fashion is what one *wears* oneself. What is unfashionable is what other people *wear*. OSCAR WILDE
6. Three Scotsmen were visiting London for a holiday and on Sunday they went to church. As the collection plate moved closer, they became more and more worried. Just before the plate reached them, one of the Scotsmen fainted and the other two *carried* him out of the church.

TASK 6: A quiz on the company

1. The gentleman here will check our passes.	Main gate
2. These young ladies welcome our visitors and show them to the right room.	Reception
3. On our right we can have a tea or coffee.	Canteen
4. Over there we store the finished products.	Warehouse
5. Here you can see how the components are put together.	Assembly area
6. The company cars are over there. One of our chauffeurs will drive you back to the station.	Transport pool
7. My colleagues here are on the look out for new products and new markets.	Marketing Department
8. The gentlemen in this building are responsible for innovation.	Research & Development Department
9. The chaps on the third floor watch over the budgets.	Finance Department
10. On the second floor they buy the components for the scales.	Purchasing Department
11. Through the glass door you can watch the guys who try to get rid of our products.	Sales Department
12. These people tell customers how good our products are.	Advertising Department
13. They know how to handle the angry customers and their problems.	Customer Service
14. Those people in uniforms watch over our safety and security day and night.	Security Service
15. And these charming young ladies provide us with stationery and sometimes type our papers.	General office
16. These gentlemen sit at expensive desks at the carpet level and smoke Havannas.	Members of the Board
17. This charming smart lady is the workhorse of the company. She organises the boss.	Executive Secretary

CHAPTER 16

TASK 1: Key words in business

eine Produktreihe ergänzen	*complement* a product range
die Umsätze zweier Firmen vereinen	*combine* the *turnovers* of two companies
Vertreter der Gewerkschaft	*trade union* representatives
einen vollen Terminkalender haben	have a very *busy* schedule
Das Personal ist der größte Vermögensposten einer Firma.	The staff is the greatest *asset* of a company.
Wir nennen es natürliche Abgänge.	We call it *natural wastage.*
Die Veränderungen werden sich auf uns auswirken.	The changes are going to *affect* us.

TASK 2: Pitfalls for Germans

Tricky words

1. What I can say is that this *merger* is in the best interests of both companies.
   fusion: Verschmelzung von Atomkernen
2. There are no *recipes* for every situation.
   receipt: Quittung
   prescription: Rezept, das der Arzt verschreibt
   recipe: Koch- und andere Rezepte
3. And I am the first person to say that this is a very *unpleasant / inconvenient* situation.
   uncomfortable: unbequem im physischen Sinn
4. It is clear to me that you are very *committed on behalf* of the workforce.
   engaged: verlobt
5. I cannot *sign* a sheet of paper which promises you things I cannot implement.
   underwrite a risk: ein Risiko versichern
6. Some of your *personnel* will leave the company.
   personal: persönlich

Tricky Grammar

7. We are *all* in the same boat. (idiomatischer Ausdruck)

   Sitting ist falsch, denn spricht man von einem Dauerzustand, verwendet man *simple tense*. Spricht man von einem vorübergehenden Tätigkeit, nimmt man *progressive tense.*

8. You know just *as well as I do* that ...

   Sie wissen genauso *gut* wie ich, dass ...
   Gut ist hier Adverb, deshalb *well* und nicht *good.*
   He's as tall *as* I am.
   Beim Vergleich mit *as* wird das Verb durch eine Form von *do* oder *be* wieder aufgenommen.

TASK 3: Test your memory

1. Why did Tissmann not meet Bloggs earlier?
   He has had a very busy schedule.
2. Why is Bloggs afraid of parallel work?
   Parallel work means job losses. People will be doing the same jobs.
3. What does Tissmann understand by 'natural wastage'?
   Some of the staff will retire. They will not be replaced. In this way they can get numbers down.

TASK 4: Beef up your word power

set on staff	*lay off* staff
hire workers	*fire* workers
employ a secretary	*dismiss* a secretary

TASK 5: Joke your way round trouble spots

1. **C.** commitment   **B.** dedication
2. **A.** engagement
3. **A.** engaged
4. **B.** sign
5. **A.** underwrite

TASK 6: More pitfalls to joke around

1. **A.** unpleasant **B.** embarrassing
2. **C.** receipts
3. **B.** co-operation
4. **B.** uncomfortable
5. **A.** contribution
6. **A.** fusion **B.** fission (Spaltung)
7. **B.** takeover

TASK 7: Two more tricky words

"Can you do shorthand?" asked the *Personnel* Manager.
"Yes, but it takes me longer," answered the young secretary.

When the boss came into the office fifteen minutes early one morning, he surprised the office manager locked in fond embrace with his *personal* assistant.

CHAPTER 17

TASK 1: Pitfalls for Germans

Tricky grammar

1. *So will I* – Ich auch.
   Nach *so* wird das Hilfsverb (*do, be, have*) in der gleichen Zeit wiederholt. Vollverben werden durch eine Form von *do* ersetzt:
   I *met* Peter the other day. – So *did* I.
2. I'll certainly suggest to the Board *that they send* 2000 of the Pulsometers.
   I *suggest going* to the theatre. Der Sprecher schließt sich in den Vorschlag mit ein.
   I suggest *that* you *go* to the cinema. Mit *suggest that* ... macht der Sprecher anderen einen Vorschlag und kann sich ausschließen.

Tricky phrases

3. *When* I was living in Germany I never ever played golf.
   As am Satzanfang bedeutet *während*, oder *da*, nicht *als*.
   Aber: *As* a teacher you should know better. Als Lehrer ...
4. Oh, *in our country* it's much too expensive.
5. Thanks for the copy of this fiscal year's *balance sheet* that you sent me.
   Bilanz: balance sheet
6. The *rate* of the *Euro* to the pound is so low.
   Wechselkurs: *exchange rate*;
   course: Kurs (Navigation); *in the course of time*: im Laufe der Zeit
7. I'm sure you'll soon *be in the black* again.
8. Well, actually I was thinking of *taking / spending a holiday* in Portugal at a golf hotel.
   Merke: *you take a holiday,* aber *you're a holiday-maker* und *you go on holiday* (ohne Artikel).

TASK 2: Joke your way round trouble spots

1. "You might as well come, *too*."
2. They had pollution in the old days, *too* ...
3. *So* does torture.
4. "Now beam down my clothes *as well / too*."
5. "They may *also* be used for hats and coats."
6. Our clothes not only make girls slim, they *also* make men look round.

TASK 3: More trouble spots to joke around

1. "Hey, Fritz, do we still take dollars at today's (exchange) *rate*?"
2. John Smith was a second *rate* author.
3. Insurance: paying for catastrophes on the *instalment* plan.
4. One Saturday afternoon, there was a commotion on the golf *course* ...
5. John, having completed a *course* of analysis with his psychiatrist ...
6. We're investigating the matter and will advise you in due *course*.